Wholeness

God's Plan For
Restoring Broken Relationships

By Dr. Jim and Malinda Uhlenkott

Contents

Preface

Life is hard. Sometimes, it feels like there is no hope at all, as if there's a huge hole within us, and the desperation just keeps growing inside. Anxiety and hopelessness build to the point where we can feel trapped and overcome by a world glutted with conflict and disappointments.

It doesn't have to be this way. The HOLE deep within can be filled and we can lead rich, satisfying and contented lives. Damaged and broken relationships are often at the core of the confusion, depression and irritation that we suffer. Battles within our marriages, conflicts at work or at home, raging arguments with people we love or a complete shutdown of communication all can be sourced to our inability to navigate through stressful circumstances in a constructive and successful way.

Wholeness speaks to where so many of us already live: right in the middle of difficult and often painful relationships. But there is hope. God has provided a proven model that makes it possible for us to work through these challenges. This book explains the very method given to mankind from the beginning. Using clear modern life examples, Wholeness provides a successful approach for loving others and ourselves while we move through life's complicated relationship problems.

1. I Can't Take It Anymore

Mark

Mark sat at the table looking down at his food while they went at it. Again. His mom and dad were having another fight, but this one was more volatile than the others. Names were being called and words being used that hadn't been a part of the usual spats that were all too common to the teenage boy. This one was getting nasty. He thought he was used to it; after all, these fights had been a part of his life for as long as he could remember, but he wasn't. He never got used to it. It hurt every time. His heart would pound in his chest, sweat would break out on his forehead, and he longed for a place of escape. He often thought about running away, but he was too realistic for that. He had no place to go. He finished his meal, or most of it, took his dishes into the kitchen and went up to his room. They didn't even appear to notice that he had left.

Life. It can be so hard. Sometimes, perhaps most of the time for some people, it feels that there is no hope. Nothing is ever going to change. We've tried to make things work; we've tried to work through problems and deal with people but to no avail. People. That's the real problem. Working with people can be an exercise in futility. They can be selfish, arrogant, mean and vindictive. Living with them is even worse. There's no place to run, nowhere to escape, no place of solitude. For every one nice person we encounter it seems as if there are twenty who are only out for themselves. If we just didn't have to be around people.

We have all been here. We have all been where Mark is. We are stuck in situations that we didn't create and that we can't solve. Life wouldn't be this tough if people would just get their acts together! Why can't people just get along? These feelings can be especially true in the one place we should feel the safest and most secure: the family.

The family is where people grow up together, see each other daily, and know each other the best. The smallest personality traits, likes, dislikes, quirks and idiosyncrasies are known by all. This close familiarity combined with the love of family members one to another should produce relationships that are caring and loving. This should be where people extend the most love, patience and understanding. Unfortunately, this isn't always the case. This familiarity, this closeness that should produce strong bonds of love and affection, is also the breeding ground for miscommunication and misunderstanding. The close bonds of family, when joined with difficult relationships born out of misinterpretation or unresolved conflict can leave us feeling frustrated, hurt, and even trapped. Spouses, family members, or people of all ages can feel ensnared in a situation from which they feel there is no escape. They may believe there are no choices to make. There is no reprieve. Nothing will fix this. These are the emotions of hopelessness.

Hopelessness brings desperation and confusion. It weakens our ability to evaluate what is true from what is subjective. Problem solving is more difficult when we feel hopeless. Our ability to view situations objectively and to problem-solve effectively is weakened. What we once may have viewed as a mistake in judgment or a poor decision on the part of someone else now gets viewed as a personal attack. Matters are made worse when the action of someone else is indeed a personal attack.

Unresolved conflict is an emotional trigger. We are designed to deal with conflict directly, honestly, and in a timely manner. Our brains are made to seek resolutions to conflicts and when this does not happen, our emotions get triggered. If the conflict is prolonged, the emotions of confusion and anger rise in us. These emotions cloud our judgment, making it difficult to view the situation accurately and to problem-solve toward a solution. The facts become confused and our feelings toward the other person change from positive to negative, or from loving to vengeful. We may lash out in our hurt, saying things not to clarify but to inflict pain. Or, perhaps worse, we just give up, withdraw, and find someplace to hide.

Mark and his parents are dealing with these emotions. The mom and dad are affected by the unresolved conflict between them. Their inability to resolve this conflict has triggered strong emotions, making it difficult for either of them to see the conflict clearly. Words that should have been used to seek understanding and resolution are now used to cause damage and pain. The parents are hurting each other, but they are also hurting Mark. The words spoken between the parents, while hurtful and damaging, are not the biggest source of pain for Mark. The environment of conflict, the atmosphere of anger is an ever-present companion to Mark. He lives with this and takes it with him wherever he goes. It is the source of his hopelessness, affecting all of his emotions, his decision making, and likely his physical and mental health.[1] He may not even hear the words any more. They aren't needed. The anger between his parents is tangible.

Our response during these times of hopelessness is often to find the quickest and easiest way out. It is our "fight or flight" syndrome kicking in. We may want to just run away, leave, or do anything that will just get us out of the situation. If we can find a way out of this conflict then we can get on with our lives. We can feel that life would be better if we didn't have conflict.

The problem is that this is not true. We are made to deal with conflict.

Noted researcher and associate professor of psychiatry at Harvard Medical School Dr. John Ratey writes that mental and emotional stress can not only be dealt with effectively, it can be healthy. In his book *Spark; The Revolutionary New Science of Exercise and the Brain*, Ratey writes "...stress seems to have an effect on the brain similar to that of vaccines on the immune system."[2] If the stress is not too severe, and if the neurons have ample time to recover, the synaptic connections in our brain are actually strengthened. If the stress is severe or chronic and unrelenting, meaning there is no time for recovery, then our brains respond just like our bodies: continual breakdown, weakening and deterioration. The effects of chronic stress can produce weight gain, insulin resistance and possibly diabetes, panic attacks, anxiety, depression and increased risk of heart disease.

We are the only species that has the mental and emotional tools for complex, interpersonal and emotional conflict resolution. These tools need development and nurturing but they exist in all of us. In fact, the strong emotions we feel during conflict are healthy. They are a sign that our feelings and emotions are intact. We hurt because we have not closed ourselves off to others. We are allowing ourselves to affect and be affected by others. We are

---

[1] Cummings, et all, 1985.

[2] Ratey, 2008

created by God to be emotional beings and conflict tells us that these emotions are alive and well. It is possible that we reflect God's image the most when we are emotional.

Relational problems, poor decision-making and poor communications have been present since man was created. Adam and Eve, God's first couple, were placed in a special garden made just for them, and still had issues.[3] While walking and talking with God in paradise, the first couple made decisions that disrupted the most loving, caring relationship that ever existed, didn't talk about it until it was too late, and, when confronted, blamed someone else.[4] This all happened in paradise, between two people who were literally "made for each other", with no bosses, deadlines, in-laws, budget cuts, high mortgage payments, gas prices or other outside influences to cause conflict between them. Not only did this first couple disobey God, they disrespected each other.

Why would Adam and Eve make such a horrible decision and disobey the only commandment God gave them? Our human condition, with its proclivity for self-indulgence, caused conflict from the very beginning.

Some people say that this first couple was overcome by evil; they were "forced" into this decision by the lie told them by the serpent. True, they were lied to, but their decision was not the result of being "forced" into something. The serpent spoke to them. Nothing more. There was no physical, emotional or spiritual force put on them. They had the capability to listen or not, to act or not. People, God's most precious creation, from the beginning of time have been given freedom to make decisions – good or bad.

Did Adam and Eve experience internal conflict before they made their decision to disobey God? Was there conflict between them over something one of them had said or done before? Did they get into an argument that morning? It's possible, perhaps even likely. Either one of them could have said or done something that was less than kind, or was interpreted incorrectly by the other. It's possible that unresolved conflict existed and clouded their judgment.

---

[3] Gen. 2:7-25

[4] Gen. 3:1-24

We encounter things in our lives that do not have easy answers and are difficult to deal with. Many of these involve other people, often complicating things dramatically. No man or woman, from the first people ever created, has lived life without problems.

We are emotional beings and as such we are going to respond to situations emotionally. As much as we would like to observe and deal with difficult situations with pure objectivism, we can't. Human emotions are a vital and integral part of our world and it is only by recognizing and understanding the emotional responses of others and ourselves that we can have success in our relationships.

It begins by understanding and facing our own internal issues, our strengths, weaknesses, desires and emotions. When we realize that all these thoughts and feelings have value and purpose, not only for our lives but also for those around us, we cannot only accept them but embrace them. The very areas that we may think are horrible, ugly and ungodly may be the very things that have been put in us to reflect a special part of God. It can be hard to imagine until that area has been "cleaned up" a little to see its value and beauty.

Our emotions have value. God has placed the things we feel deep inside in us. The first place we can look to help us through difficult relationships is at those very personal places that bring us the most pain.

The Bible refers to these deep inner places as the heart, soul and mind.[5] Other translations, however, would be the heart and reins (kidneys).[6] At first glance the words *heart* and *kidneys* don't appear to be very accurate terms to describe our emotions. A closer inspection, however, shows that these words provide a very good picture of the workings of our inner emotions. The heart and kidneys are directly involved with the very source of life and health. It is the proper functioning of these vital organs that allows our bodies to operate as they should. Without them we cease to exist. Our emotions function the same way. They make it possible for us to feel joy, pain, empathy, gladness and sorrow. These are the feelings of life. If we lose the proper functioning of these feelings we may still be operational but we won't be relational. The reference to the heart and kidneys is a very apt description indeed and it allows

---

[5] Jer. 17:10

[6] Ps. 7:9, KJV, Ps. 73:21,KJV

us to gain better insight into the ways God designed human beings to interact in our relationships to each other.

It's true that our emotions are very powerful and can make it difficult to see situations clearly, but they can also be useful tools for reconciliation. Knowing and understanding our emotions, their triggers, the reactions they produce, their potential for great love and concern, and for great anger, is what equips us to understand the emotions of others. This understanding of our emotions is the source of empathy. Without them we are incapable of knowing the struggles and difficulties of others, incapable of loving others when they are hurting, and incapable of helping. We sometimes wish that we weren't so emotional, or perhaps that others weren't so emotional. We may try to keep our emotions in check or to be void of them altogether. Relationships lacking emotions also lack the life and vitality that make them so special.

Our decisions are formed far more often out of our inner feelings, out of our emotions, than out of logic or empirical evidence. Decisions ranging from what we have for dinner to where we live and what job we take are highly influenced by how we "feel." This does not make us weak, uneducated or foolish. It makes us human. We are made in God's image, and God is emotional. He expressed joy, anger, love, compassion and grief. Rejecting this part of our nature is to reject God and the way He made us. We are not to reject, hide or neglect our emotions; we are to rule over them. God's glory is seen in us being fully human, the way He created us, and He created us with emotions. Understanding this valuable part of our God-given nature enables us to learn to effectively manage our emotions.

We are complicated beings with strong emotions. These emotions affect every aspect of our lives including, and perhaps especially, our closest relationships. These emotions often seem to complicate our interactions as opposed to making them better, and cause problems than we might not have without them. It is easy to view our emotions, and especially the emotions of others, as sources of problems rather than parts of the solution. If only people weren't so emotional. These complicated and complex emotions, these challenging, hard to explain, illogical feelings that seem to surface when we need them the least, can also be the very source of help and even healing. They can help us learn how to communicate honestly and openly. They can teach us more about ourselves and equip us to understand others.

He lay on his bed, staring at the ceiling. How long could he put up with this? It hurt so badly. He loved his parents, but at times like this he hated them, or at least he hated what they did to him. Why couldn't he have been born into a normal family? His friends' parents didn't fight like this; they didn't yell at each other and call each other horrible names. Why did his parents act this way?

2. Who Can I Blame?

Steve

The note said it all but said nothing. "I want a divorce." written in black letters on a plain piece of paper changed Steve's life forever. This couldn't be happening. Should he have seen this coming? How did he miss the signs? Things were going just fine for them. Evidently they weren't. He sat down on the couch, staring at the paper, hoping the words would somehow disappear.

"This isn't all my fault, you know!" He spoke the words out loud, as if she could hear him from wherever she had gone after leaving what was once their home. He replayed different scenes from their years together; each neatly selected and edited to fuel the anger building inside him. He had felt controlled and put down by her from the beginning. Nothing he did was ever good enough. She was constantly telling him how to do things, where to put things, what he had to do that day. He had laid down his pride for her over and over again, willing to take her constant mothering because he loved her. Evidently that wasn't enough. This was not all his fault!

Life doesn't happen in a vacuum and our actions affect not only those that are in relationship with us, but also those around us. We may find it easiest to blame others when things fall apart. It makes life a little easier to think that the messes we find ourselves in are not all of our own doing. This mess can't be our entire fault and sometimes, it really isn't.

Whether something happens to us or because of us, our emotions get triggered. There are many responses besides wanting to blame others. Sometimes we feel anger, resentment, jealousy or hopelessness. What can a person do that feels trapped in a world they didn't create?

Our human nature is equipped to respond to situations in emotional ways. There are a variety of emotional responses and they are not always helpful. Jealousy makes us want something, anything that someone else has that we don't. Anger hopes to change the situation through a strong emotional response, or to lash out at someone or something physically. Self-pity thinks that if everyone knew how hard it is for us then our plight would get easier. Resentment brings displeasure or indignation over what someone has done or said. Fear is sometimes the most aggressive emotion that threatens to make anything and everything worse than it really is. These emotions are not inherently bad; on the contrary they can be effective and useful as we navigate through the sea of our relationships, but we need wisdom and knowledge to use them effectively.

Blame can be a very pleasant emotion. It can make us feel better to think our pain was caused by someone else, instead of being self-inflicted. It takes a great load off our shoulders to know we won't have to face any embarrassment or consequences for the problems we're facing. We can feel relieved when we find someone or something to blame for our painful situations. In the story of the first family we see how quickly Adam and Eve befriended blame when they were caught in their defiance.

And He said, "Who told you that you were naked? Have you eaten from the tree from which I commanded you not to eat?" The man said, "The women whom You gave to be with me, she gave me from the tree and I ate." Then the Lord said to the woman, "What is this you have done?" And the woman said, "The serpent deceived me and I ate." (Gen. 3:11-13, NAS)

The first response from Adam and Eve when confronted about their disobedience was to blame someone else. Adam blames Eve. Eve blames the serpent. Neither of them took ownership for their actions. Our human nature is to shift the blame onto some other person or circumstance. This blame-shifting response is an attempt to deflect the focus off ourselves and onto someone or something else. Adam and Eve felt the emotion of fear, and instead of using it to examine the situation to find truth they allowed it to influence them to blame someone else. This shifting of blame did not relieve them from any of the outcomes of their actions. They were still held responsible and still suffered the consequences. Unfortunately, so did their children.

14

Cain and Abel were not born in paradise[7]; they were born outside of paradise, where ...*thorns and thistles grow...*[8] Their life was hard. They had to live by the ...*sweat of their brow...*[9] They probably heard stories of the special garden built for their mom and dad. The walks with God in the cool of the evening could have seemed like a fairy tale to the two boys as they heard about them from their parents. It would seem only natural for the boys to have some anger or resentment toward their parents for what had happened. The mistake of Adam and Eve meant a lifetime of hard work and struggle for their children and everyone that followed.

Abel, the second son, was in a difficult situation that was not his fault. He wasn't the one that disobeyed God, and yet he was suffering the consequences. Clearly, he had several people he could blame for his life's situation. The easiest would be to blame his parents.

Parenting. Perhaps the most important job we will ever have and the one that comes with very little training. All parents, no matter how good, make mistakes. All of us who have raised children can look back at specific situations, perhaps many of them, and wish we could do them over again. We wish we could take back that word or phrase, make a different decision or listen a little bit better. All of our children could blame us for something if they wanted to. Abel is no different.

The first thing Abel could have blamed his parents for was his name. "Abel" means *emptiness, vanity,* or *unsatisfactory.*[10] How would you like that hanging around your neck? Every time someone calls his name they are reminding him that this is how his parents must see him. He is the empty and vain one, the one that is unsatisfactory and will never measure up. He may have felt a huge hole in his heart, without anyone pointing it out. His brother, on the other hand, had a much different name. Cain is the older brother, the firstborn. How did his parents name him? "Cain" means *spear,* or *to strike.*[11] Now that's a

---

[7] Gen. 4:1-2
[8] Gen. 3:18
[9] Gen. 3:19
[10] Strong's Hebrew and Greek Dictionary: H1893
[11] Strong's Hebrew and Greek Dictionary: H7014

cool name! It's a name of strength and virility. A man's name! A name filled with hope and purpose.

If Abel did not blame his parents he could have always gone to the one many of us blame when there's no one else left: he could have blamed God. This is where we often go when bad things happen that are beyond our understanding. We ask the question that has been asked for perhaps centuries: why would a loving God allow... and we fill in the blank. Was God to blame? Had God set his parents up for failure in the first place? There is no shortage of candidates for Abel to focus blame upon for his situation.

Who should receive the blame? Who really is at fault? Let's look at the one most people blame: the serpent.

Now the serpent was more crafty than any beast of the field, which the Lord God had made. And he said to the woman, "Indeed, has God said, 'You shall not eat from any tree of the garden?" *And the women said to the serpent, "Of the fruit of the trees of the garden we may eat, but from the fruit of the tree which is in the middle of the garden, God has said, 'You shall not eat from it or touch it, or you will die.'" The serpent said to the woman, "You surely will not die! For God knows that in the day you eat from it your eyes will be opened, and you will be like God, knowing good and evil."* (Gen. 3:1-5, NAS)

The serpent is the easiest one to blame for all of our problems. Man was living in paradise, walking and talking with God before it showed up. It is easy to argue that Eve would never have eaten the fruit of that tree if it hadn't been for the serpent. Clearly the serpent is evil and is deserving of blame. God punishes it severely for enticing Eve. We should never underestimate or be naïve to the ways of evil, but all of the responsibility for Adam and Eve's disobedience cannot be placed solely on the serpent.

What power did the serpent have over Eve? Were Eve's actions a result of a curse or a spell being placed on her through the serpent's words? Was she made by the serpent to pick and then eat the fruit? No. The serpent talked to her, nothing more. Eve made the choice first to engage the serpent in conversation and then to give credence to its words. Eve made the choice to choose the fruit over God's explicit command against it.

There is still more blame to be found. Eve was not the only one that encountered the serpent on that day.

*And when the woman saw that the tree was good for food, and that it was a delight to the eyes, and that the tree was to be desired to make one wise, she took of the fruit thereof, and did eat; and **she gave also unto her husband with her** and he did eat.* (Emphasis added) (Gen. 3:6 NAS)

It appears from this scripture that Adam was with Eve, perhaps standing right next to her, while the serpent was talking to her, hearing the lies and falsehoods coming from its mouth, and he did nothing to stop it.

Adam should have grabbed a club and threatened to make a pair of boots out of the serpent unless he left his wife alone! He should have driven it out of the garden as soon as it spoke, but he didn't. He listened, he remained silent, and he joined his wife in eating the forbidden fruit. Why? Why didn't Adam take action? Adam was a man that experienced what no man has before or since: he walked and talked with God Himself. He had access to the very source of all knowledge. It is reasonable to think that Adam had wonderful conversations with God and asked questions and received divine answers.[12] Adam received from God "...a great capacity and suitable propensity to increase in knowledge..."[13] This tree, however, this one and only tree from which he could not eat the fruit of, could give him knowledge he didn't have: the knowledge of evil. He had the source of knowledge of good at his disposal at any time. He knew God and so knew all that was good and pure. The knowledge of evil, however, was unknown to him. Perhaps this was what enticed him to let down his guard and stand with Eve as she engaged in a conversation with the serpent. Evil is a powerful source. Its dark nature fills us with intrigue and mystery, and we are drawn to its unknown qualities.

---

[12] Albert Barnes' Notes on the Bible
[13] Adam Clarke's Commentary on the Bible

Both Adam and Eve had the opportunity to resist the temptation before them. Either one of them could have said, "No. I'm not doing this." But they didn't, and when confronted by God neither of them took responsibility for their actions. They both blamed someone else.

It appears this propensity of ours to blame others has been part of our human nature from the beginning.

Steve stared at the note again. What was behind these words of wanting a divorce? He wondered if someone had enticed his wife into a relationship. He knew she was friendly with several guys at work, but he hadn't ever thought about any of them causing his marriage to be destroyed. Would she have been lured by some cheap talk or sultry come-ons? His mind raced to find an answer. He tried to imagine all the possible scenarios that could have led his wife to this decision. There had to be a reason! She wouldn't just leave without one! Who did this to him?

Perhaps the real issue is not who is at fault, or whether or not there is evil in the world, or why bad things happen to good people. The issue is not the problems that we face but how we respond to these problems when they happen. Our troubles may come from many sources that are clearly wrong or evil, but we are free to choose how to respond to every situation. God gave us that freedom. God did not create us to be puppets for His control or anyone else's. We are free to decide how we will speak, act and react.

3. Finding Truth

Steve

Steve placed the note down on the table and walked away. He was moving on, and this physical act of placing the note back on the table, this small piece of paper that had just ruined his life, and walking away from it was his first step. He could do this; after all, she did. She walked away without as much as a single word to him. She didn't have the guts, or the decency, to talk to him face-to-face. Fine. If she could do it, so could he. Only he couldn't. He stopped, turned, and faced the note, looking at its words, "I want a divorce.". This was more than just a declarative statement. Far greater things were contained in these four words. This note was an accusation; it accused him of being a poor husband, a poor companion and lover. It was a pejorative statement on his character. It was the verdict handed to a judge by the jury foreman pronouncing him guilty of failing in his duties to his wife. Was it all true? Was he that man? It couldn't be true, could it? What was true?

Truth. It appears to be a difficult concept. It can seem illusive, vague, difficult to define, open to debate and subjective. It is the source of theological, political and philosophical debates. Books, articles, conferences and university courses seek to extol upon its virtues and/or its complexities. We seek it for ourselves and others, often through a variety of sources and multiple methods. Attempting to find agreement on the nature and meaning of truth can be an exercise in futility, ranging from heated arguments at family gatherings to seemingly insurmountable political divisions. Yet we still seek it.

Why? Why do we pursue such an elusive concept so assiduously? What drives us to know truth and to want others to know it as well? Is it really that difficult to define and understand? As with all concepts, perspective is everything.

Our view of the world and its "truths" as we know them is defined by our perspective, the lens through which we see the world. This lens is custom-made, formed specifically for us by our experiences, education, gender, age, upbringing, family relations, work experiences and everything else that we've encountered throughout our lives. It is through this personally designed optical glass that we evaluate, assess and pass judgment on everything we encounter. Our perspective is built, adjusted, tested and readjusted through every encounter and experience. Another term for this perspective is "schema."

Since no two people have the exact same experiences, no two people have the exact same schema; not friends, not family members, not coworkers, not spouses. Even identical twins that have the exact same DNA have different schemas because they have each had different experiences with friends, family members, jobs and so on. Our quest for truth runs through the highway of our schema, our perspective.

He was a good husband! He was a good father! What was her problem? Steve thought back through their married life, replaying the scenes in his head. What did she have to complain about? He treated her well, cared for her, showed his love for her and always provided for her. If anything, he had more to complain about than she did! What was she thinking?

Steve believed he had been a good husband, but obviously his wife thought otherwise. He knew the things she would probably bring up: he didn't talk enough, he didn't do things her way, he's too strict with the kids. He wanted to know the truth. He picked up his phone and dialed.

Our perspectives, although similar in many areas to those of others, are unique, and since they are unique, our definitions and understandings of what is true are unique as well. There may be truths that seem universal, that we all seem to agree on, but even these "truths" are open to interpretation under the right circumstances. We may all agree that lying and stealing are wrong, but we also might choose to engage in either or both if placed in very specific and/or difficult situations.

The search for truth is a search through other perspectives. It is only effective if we are willing to look at situations through someone else's lens. One such lens is that of the Bible. What does it say about truth?

The Hebrew word for truth is *"emeth"*[14] and its primary meaning is stability. The search for truth is a search for constancy and firm foundations. We all desire a strong base for our beliefs and values and we search for truth, this source of consistency, in many areas, some of which provide us with some measure of security. This security is often fleeting, however, and we move on to the next best-selling book or the next guest on the talk show providing their view of truth. There is only one true source of truth, and that is God. God's truth is the source of stability in our lives and the world in which we live.

Knowing and understanding God's truth, however, is often, perhaps usually, more difficult than trying to understand a friend's or a spouse's. We may study it, meditate on it, and even try to live by it, but the words from 1 Corinthians 13:9 will always apply: *"...we know in part."* Our attempt to know and understand God's Word and His ways is a life-long journey, full of course-altering corrections, but a journey that is necessary if we are to be whole people, able to live with and love His people.

It is only through God's truth that the world makes sense. It brings clarity to that which is vague; it shines light on what appears to be dark and hidden; it brings firmness to areas that are unstable. God designed all of mankind to rule, and to do that we must find truth from which to rule. We need to see what is real when everything appears dark and hidden; we need firmness when areas feel unstable. Truth brings stability into a world of inconsistencies. Without it every personal interpretation becomes correct, and instead of leadership we have chaos. It is no wonder, then, that the first plan of evil against God's creation was about what is true.

Now the serpent was craftier than any beast of the field, which the LORD God had made. And he said to the woman, "Indeed, has God said, 'You shall not eat from any tree of the garden'?" [2] The woman said to the serpent, "From the fruit of the trees of the garden we may eat; [3] but from the fruit of the tree which is in the middle of the garden, God has said, 'You shall not eat from it or touch it, or you will die.'" [4] The serpent said to the woman, "You surely will not die! [5] For God knows that in the day you eat from it your eyes will be opened, and you will be like God, knowing good and evil." (Gen. 3:1-5, NAS)

---

[14] Strong's Hebrew and Greek Dictionary: H571

As was pointed out in chapter two, Eve's first mistake was engaging the serpent in conversation. The serpent can do nothing if it is ignored. It has no power to force Eve to eat the forbidden fruit, or to even talk about it. Since the serpent has no power over Eve, it must use something to entice Eve into a conversation. And it does. The serpent approaches Eve casually, with familiarity and with agreement.

Familiarity. It is the state of being familiar and close. Familiarity exists between close friends, family members and spouses. It is the bond of close relationships, where we are so familiar with someone that we can predict their next action or words. There is no ceremony, no pomp or formality with those with whom we are familiar. Social etiquettes are eschewed and liberties are taken freely. The serpent approaches Eve in this manner, as one friend would approach another. In doing so the serpent presents no obvious threat; there is no need for Eve to raise her defenses. This animal is friendly, and this is just a conversation. The serpent's attempt to approach Eve as someone with whom she can identify and be familiar with is seen it its first words.

The serpent's first word is "indeed," or in some translations, "yea." The serpent uses two Hebrew words, first, "*aph*"[15]: a word of agreement, of acknowledgment, the equivalent of accession, consent, and agreement. The second word is "*kiy*"[16] which indicates a casual relationship.

Why would you begin a conversation this way? It is an attempt to approach Eve casually, as a friend, and to agree with what she is already thinking. These two words also denote an interrogative surprise. Our modern vernacular would sound something like this: "Really? God said you can't eat from <u>any</u> tree in the garden?" These two words were chosen by the serpent with purpose and precision, allowing it to be familiar to Eve, to join Eve in her emotional dilemma (Why would God restrict us from this one tree? It makes no sense!). It finds common emotional ground upon which both it and Eve can stand. It is from this common ground that the lie can be presented. Was Eve standing by the tree of the knowledge of good and evil, staring at the fruit when the serpent approached? Did the serpent see her staring at it, wondering about it,

---

[15] Strong's Hebrew and Greek Dictionary: H637
[16] Strong's Hebrew and Greek Dictionary: H3588

and then agree with her thoughts? *Indeed, has God said, "You will not eat from any tree of the garden?"* We don't know, but the words chosen by the serpent in its approach to Eve indicate that Eve was certainly thinking about God's restriction and probably feeling it was a bit too restrictive. So the serpent approaches her casually, as a friend, and draws out of her what she must have been already thinking.

The serpent takes this familiarity one step further. Not only does it speak to Eve in this manner, it speaks of God the same way.

The serpent asks a question: *Indeed, has God said, "You will not eat from any tree of the garden?"* Again, the serpent chooses its words to fit its purpose, that purpose being to reduce God's position and stature in the eyes of Eve.

The word the serpent uses for God is *"elohiym."*[17] This term does not speak of God as the One Who Was, Is, and Always Will Be. It does not refer to the Alpha and Omega, the Creator of the Universe. This word isn't even about <u>one</u> god. The word is plural; the word for many gods, and the word is informal, speaking of ordinary gods. The word is also used for rulers and judges or even public officials. The serpent's question not only dares to question God's command to His people, it plants the seed of disrespect into Eve. How do we know this? Because Eve answers the serpent with the same word.

The woman said to the serpent, "From the fruit of the trees of the garden we may eat; but from the fruit of the tree which is in the middle of the garden, God has said, 'You shall not eat from it or touch it, or you will die.'" (Gen. 3:2-3, NAS)

Eve takes liberties with God's words and adds to them. God did not say, "or touch it". Eve did. More importantly, however, Eve joins the serpent in its disrespect, its disregard for God. Eve uses the same word, *"elohiym"* in her answer, choosing to describe God in the same manner as the serpent, as one god among many. She reduced God, her creator, to that of a judge or ruler. The supremacy of God is now reduced to casual acknowledgment. She reduced God relationally, from the One that created, loved and cared for her to one that

---

[17] Strong's Hebrew and Greek Dictionary: H430

just makes rules. She changed her relationship with God through her choice of words.

The serpent is successful in its attempt to get Eve to think about God in casual terms. Now that Eve is on much more even terms with God, questioning His words and even His motives is not too difficult. The serpent and Eve are now on the same page, in agreement that God is not so great, and that perhaps His command has some ulterior motive.

The serpent said to the woman, "You surely will not die! For God knows that in the day you eat from it your eyes will be opened, and you will be like God, knowing good and evil." (Gen. 3:2-5, NAS)

You will be "like god, like elohiym, like all of the other gods, rulers and judges." This makes the lie even more palatable, more believable. Eve may have trouble believing that she can turn into the one, true God, but perhaps it is not so difficult to think that she could become the one that makes the rules.

The lie is presented only after the serpent and Eve are in agreement. Now they are friends, joined in their common bond of questioning and distrusting God. Both the serpent and Eve have altered God's words. Eve added to them with the words, "or touch it" and the serpent exaggerates God's prohibition by adding, "...of any tree..." Now the serpent can alter God's command even further, and bring into question His motives. It is effective in its attempt to have Eve consider that God is keeping her subjugated, perhaps enslaved, keeping her from becoming important or independent. The distrust of God is born. The disobedience is in sight. The relationship has changed. It becomes one of power and control instead of love and concern. She has lost any desire to care about the relationship with God, her husband or how her actions will affect them. She is focused on herself.

This distrust of God has produced the phenomenon that is usually present when we decide to trust in ourselves instead of in Him: imaginary liberty. Eve is told the lie that if she eats the forbidden fruit she will be like God. What more liberty can there be? She can be like God, the Creator, knowing all and able to do all. She, like us, is enthralled by the possibilities, the freedoms and the power. It is imaginary, however. There is no real liberty in a life without God. Real liberty is only found in recognizing who and what we are: God's loved creation. True liberty and freedom is relational. It doesn't come from a lack of rules, but from finding peace and stability where you live. A person that has isolated themselves from all relationships and responsibilities in life hasn't found freedom, just purposelessness and seclusion. This doesn't mean that we won't find ourselves in situations that are unjust. People can be controlling, insensitive and uncaring. These are situations to work through, not run from.

Eve's response to the lie of the serpent is to speak truth, but only to the point that it benefits her. The truth is changed, edited to her best advantage. God has been reduced and devalued. She listened to the serpent instead of turning away. She was aware of God's command and its purpose, but she proved by her exaggeration of God's words that she believed it to be too restrictive. Her love and confidence in God were wavering before the serpent ever showed up.

Eve doubted God and His care for her. She doubted His motives. It is easy to think that this was her sin: that she doubted God. It wasn't. Because our understanding of truth is a product of our perspective it is important to have that perspective either confirmed or proved false. We do this by asking questions, seeking information, and even by doubting. Eve had questions about God's command. These questions were an opportunity for sin, but they were also an opportunity for truth. The conversation with the serpent did not have to result in disobedience; in fact, it could have led to a stronger conviction in God and His truth. Eve could have recognized the subtle word play used by the serpent. She could have identified how this touched her emotions. This could have led to an even stronger belief in her God.

It is not wrong for truth to be questioned. Truth is always going to be examined and tested. It must be in order to be accepted on a personal level. Truth cannot be put on you or given to you. If it is then it fails to be truth and becomes just a rule. For truth to work there must be personal ownership of it and belief in it. Eve did not accept, and therefore did not own, God's truth. It was just a rule. This is okay, even healthy. She could have tested this truth, asking God to explain it. She could have questioned it, as a daughter does with her father, and learned about its meaning and importance. It then would have become a truth for her to understand and live by, instead of just a rule to obey.

Love, too, should be doubted and tested to be accepted as worthy of our trust. In this way we find stability within our relationships. It is through this very same process of voicing our concerns, our irritations, and even our doubts, that our relationships become stable. The foundation for relationships cannot be that of doubt and questions, but rather the truth that comes from speaking about them, bringing them to the surface, and making a decision to deal with them.

Steve put the phone down. His wife's words were sharp. What did she mean when she said: "You don't listen. You never finish what you say you are going to do. I can't ever depend on you." Her words clouded everything he had been thinking. How could anything she said be true? How could she have such a different view on their marriage? He didn't know what to think or feel. He wanted the truth and had asked to know exactly what she was thinking, but now he was more confused than ever.

This is why the search for truth is so important. Truth can cause us to question every aspect of our lives. It can validate our knowledge; it can clarify our understanding; it can stabilize our emotions, but it can also bring doubt to each of these areas and be the impetus for self-examination. The search for truth is a constant scrutiny of our perspective and beliefs. It is a process, and it is often confrontational.

Noted Swiss psychologist Jean Piaget[18] (1896-1980) identified two basic tendencies in human thinking. The first is assimilation, in which we use our existing schema, our understanding of the world based on our collective experiences, to make sense of any new information we encounter. We use our current knowledge and understanding to assimilate, to understand and make sense of, new information.

The second basic tendency in our thinking is that of accommodation. Accommodation occurs when the new information does not align with our current schema. This new information doesn't make sense to us based on our

---

[18] Piaget, 1954, translated by Margaret Cook

current understandings. Our schema will have to be rewritten to accommodate this new "truth."

Piaget continues that our minds are always attempting to find mental equilibrium: a search for balance in our thinking and understanding. This search for mental equilibrium is innate: we are hard-wired for this and we begin this process as infants. We need things to make sense. We have "truths" that we have formed through our experiences and interactions with others. These "truths" provide us with our mental and emotional equilibrium. Without "equilibration," as Piaget terms it, we become mentally unstable. Our world can be shaken when a "truth" we have believed for years is suddenly questioned or proved to be false. There are only three choices for us whenever new information is encountered in order for us to maintain equilibration:

• Assimilation. This new "truth" is in line with our current understanding. It makes sense based on what we already believe to be true, so we assimilate. We accept this truth. We have mental equilibrium.

• Accommodation. This new truth is contrary to our current knowledge and understanding, our schema, but we see value in it and are willing to make some changes to our beliefs. Our current schema will be altered, rewritten, to accommodate this new information. Again, we have mental equilibrium.

• Rejection. We are unable to line up this new "truth" with our existing schema. It is so contrary to our beliefs that we cannot accept it. We cannot assimilate or accommodate this new information, so we reject it, allowing us to maintain mental equilibrium.

Our understanding of truth is under constant review. We engage in the three-step process described above every day, often without even realizing it. We must in order to maintain a mental balance, our mental equilibrium. Because our understanding of truth is ever growing, our perspective will be confronted when real truth is discovered. Our schema, which we believe to be true about the world, is challenged. This threat to our beliefs can cloud our vision and turn our world upside down. It can be confusing and alarming. This is especially true when this new "truth," this different perspective, is about us. We have a very specific portrait of ourselves in our mind; this portrait depicts us in a certain light, flattering in some areas and critical in others. It can be very challenging to have someone else suggest that this self-portrait is inaccurate. Relationships can become strained. We may be unwilling to accommodate this new information about ourselves. These things can't be true, or can they?

Here lies one of the purposes and great values of relationships. Close relationships are where our "truths" can be challenged and opened up for examination. The closeness of relationships can provide the perfect setting for people to raise concerns, point out issues, question motives, and provide differing perspectives, all in the context of love and concern. These private, close and sometimes intimate discussions can be the fertile soil for new personal growth. This is where our schema, especially about ourselves, can be changed. A successful, loving relationship grows out of loving the other person enough to speak the truth out of concern for their well-being

This is not license to point out the faults of others whenever we see them. Our first step should always be to look at ourselves. We should examine our motives to see if we truly have the other person's best interest at heart. Are we speaking out of love and concern or out of irritation? The former will bring freedom and strong relationships; the latter, hurt and separation.

Speaking the truth with love can be difficult. Most of us don't like confrontation, so we often don't say anything. We "tough it out" and make the best of it, only to explode someday when we can't take it anymore. We may leave or end the relationship without ever even telling the other person why. The divorce courts have a term for this: Irreconcilable Differences.

Real truth can be challenging, but it can also be healing. Relationships can be strengthened and even restored when we are willing to have our "truth" be confronted and examined, and when we love the other person enough to speak honestly. Stability will come when mental equilibrium and internal peace is felt.

"If you look for truth, you may find comfort in the end; if you look for comfort you will not get either comfort or truth, only soft soap and wishful thinking to begin, and in the end, despair." C.S. Lewis[19]

---

[19] C. S. Lewis. (n.d.). BrainyQuote.com. Retrieved May 18, 2013, from BrainyQuote.com Web site: http://www.brainyquote.com/quotes/quotes/c/cslewis141015.html

4. Freedom to Fail

Samantha

1:30 AM. Samantha's mom stared at the clock on the wall. Still not home. Where could she be? It wasn't like her to be this late, not without calling. But lately Samantha had been acting differently. She was more sullen, more brooding, not the happy girl that had brought life into the home for all these years. It was more difficult to talk with her now, she seemed to only want to hang out with her friends at the mall, and not be with the family anymore. The mom hoped, prayed, she was all right. Oh, if only she'd come home.

Choices. We make dozens of them every day, some perhaps better than others. The world is full of people making choices, many affect us; many do not. Sometimes we observe someone making what we deem to be poor choices. These poor choices are obvious to the rest of us, why aren't they obvious to the ones making them?

None of us like to fail and we don't want others to fail, especially those who we are close to. Our lives are complicated by the poor decisions, the failures of those around us. Failure, like it or not, is part of our human experience. Since we have all done it you would think we would be more understanding when those close to us make a poor decision or fail attempting the good decision they have made. Failure has been part of our human history from the very beginning. Why?

Why would God put Adam and Eve in a position to choose, when He knew they were likely to fail? God knew their hearts, desires and emotions, just as He knows ours. He knows that, given a choice, we are drawn toward whatever benefits us the most. Our natural tendency toward self-centeredness is seen from the very beginning, in childhood, where one of the first lessons we have to learn is to share our toys with others.

Educational psychology tells us that children are born *ego-centric*: self-focused and unaware of the needs, thoughts and emotions of others[20]. This is not a result of poor character, but rather because they truly are the center of all attention from the moment they're born. Beyond the cuteness factor that comes as standard equipment for a newborn, they are unable to meet any of their own needs and so must have everything done for them. Mom and Dad, and any other adults that happen to be nearby, spend most of their energy making sure these newborns are well cared for. Ego-centrism is also present because the awareness of the needs, perceptions and emotions of others must be learned. It is not innate.

Around the age of 2 or 3 children begin to develop *a theory of mind*: the understanding that we are not the center of the universe, and that others have thoughts, feelings and emotions that are unique to them and are different from their own[21]. This understanding leads us to broader concepts like sharing and cooperation, and continues to develop until the child is around the age of 10, although it can occur earlier or later in specific individuals. We never fully outgrow our self-centered ways; they show up in all of us at different times depending on the situation we find ourselves in (or how much we want something).

If we are predisposed to self-seeking behavior, then isn't God putting us in a position to fail by giving us a choice to begin with? If God loved us wouldn't He keep us sheltered from making any bad decisions? The answer is just the opposite. It is precisely because He loves us that He gave us the one thing that separates us from the rest of His creation: the freedom to fail.

The freedom to choose and to fail in our choices is what separates us from the animals, plants and microscopic life also created by God. We are the only ones that can look at a situation and decide what we're going to do; all other life forms have their decisions decided for them through instinct.

[20] Woolfolk, p. 46, 2012
[21] Woolfolk, p. 99 2012

Instinct: an inborn pattern of behavior characteristic of a species and shaped by biological necessities such as survival and reproduction[22].

A bear may make a decision to hunt for a fish rather than eat the berries in front of him, but this is not really a choice, it is a product of his instinct, his inborn pattern of behavior. The bear cannot make a decision that is contrary to his God-given nature.

Humans can. We certainly have inborn patterns of behavior shaped by biological necessities, survival and reproduction among them, the difference is that we can still choose even regarding these basic biological needs. We can choose when or if to eat or reproduce. We can choose to fast and not eat at all, going completely against our biological drive. We can, and do, make choices all the time that are not good for us, that go against our natural predispositions. It may be difficult to find someone that does not believe that smoking is bad for our health, yet people still can and do make the decision to do so. Our desires for specific indulgences may overrule our knowledge of what is best for our health.

God could have restricted Adam and Eve's choice. He could have made it so that the Tree of the Knowledge of Good and Evil was not attractive to them, or He could not have created it at all. At least He could have hidden it, but there is no record that the tree was anywhere but in plain sight, in fact the Scripture places the tree in the middle of the garden and attractive to the eye [(Gen. 2:9)]. It is possible, perhaps probable, that they walked by it every day, seeing the fruit and being tempted by it. It hardly seems fair.

Perhaps it wasn't fair, but it was loving and it was perfect.[23] God showed that He valued Adam and Eve more than the animals. A bear does not face moral decisions. It goes about its day doing only what it is directed to do through instinct. We, however, face moral decisions almost daily. God could have made us like He made the bear and the other animals, going about our lives only responding to life through instinctual impulses, but instead He made us with the greatest asset of all, the freedom to choose, and this freedom to

---

[22] Random House Dictionary
[23] Albert Barnes Notes on the Bible, 1798-1870

choose means that sometimes we will make poor choices. We are free to make mistakes.

For you were called to freedom, brethren; only do not turn your freedom into an opportunity for the flesh, but through love serve one another. (Gal. 5:13)

Act as free men, and do not use your freedom as a covering for evil, but use it as bondslaves of God. (1 Peter 2:16)

Both of these scriptures indicate that we can, if we choose to, use our freedom for something other than the purposes of God. The choice is ours.

This freedom to make choices, like most freedoms, is a dangerous thing. A poor choice by one person could have immediate and possibly long-term effects on many others. People are hurt every day; some have their life altered forever in horrible, catastrophic ways because of decisions made by others. All of us, at one level or another, have been the victim of someone's poor choice, have been hurt by others and have hurt others ourselves through poor choices we have made, but to take away free will is to make us less than human. Taking away our free will would also take away another vital human capacity: the ability to love.

Love does not exist without free will. If I am compelled to have strong emotional feelings toward someone else by my nature, by my instinct, then it is not love at all. Love only exists because we are free to feel it for and extend it toward others. If a man or woman had strong emotional feelings for their spouse or children only because they were hard-wired to have them they would not be expressing love, they would just be responding to the electronic impulses sent by the brain. We would then be no different than the animals, responding out of instinct, not out of our free will and choice. Love cannot exist without free will.

Unfortunately, hate exists for the same reason. This freedom to love that we all share also results in the freedom to hate. God could have made us unable to hate, unable to want to hurt or harm others, and this is exactly the question we ask when a loved one is hurt through the hate of someone else. God, why did you allow this to happen? Why didn't you intervene and not allow this horrible thing to take place? He could have. God could have stopped someone's action of hate, but then He wouldn't be a loving God, He'd be a controlling God.

What is the opposite of love? Is it hate? Ambivalence? Apathy? This is a difficult question to answer, but perhaps somewhere in the answer is the word "control." Having our decisions and actions controlled by someone else often, perhaps usually, brings a sharp, emotional response. Children, siblings, spouses and workers have all responded strongly and emotionally to being controlled. Children have rebelled, workers have quit and spouses walked out because someone was not allowing them the basic freedom to choose.

In order to be utilized well this freedom to choose must be accompanied by knowledge and wisdom. It is good for parents to control many of their children's decisions when they are young, in order to teach about the varied and multifaceted aspects of life they will encounter. Little by little, as they grow and mature, as they gain experience and understanding, the controls are taken off enabling more freedoms to be given.

There is a controlling nature present in all of us. While we can value and appreciate the different ways people do things and their different ways of thinking, we also are prone to the attitude that the world would be better off if people just thought like us. We pass judgment on people all the time, on their motives and actions, how they raise their children, on how they drive, how they dress and the list goes on. We use words that sound like encouragement or helpful suggestions, but really have a controlling attitude behind them: words like, "You should...", "You have to..." and "You must..." In reality I don't have to do anything. There will be consequences, some more serious than others, for whatever I choose to do or not do, but I get to make my own decisions. Perhaps two of the greatest lessons taught in the Garden of Eden were: 1) There are consequences for our actions and 2) We are free to choose what we will do.

So, yes, God could have intervened and stopped us from hurting someone else, but to do so, to take away our ability to dislike, to hate, and even to hurt one another, would also take away our ability to love. It would take away our humanity.

Samantha kept driving. She knew it was late, that her mom would be upset, but she felt she had no choice. Her best friend had showed up at the party either drunk, high or both, and she had to get her home before she hurt herself or someone else. A boyfriend breaking up with you shouldn't be this devastating, but it was to her friend. Samantha was spending almost all of her time now with her friend, hoping to help her back to solid ground, hoping to keep her from doing something really stupid. She was so concerned about her friend that she had a difficult time concentrating on anything else and it was hurting her other relationships, even with her mom. Her mom: really her best friend. Samantha never wanted to disappoint her mom, let alone disobey her, but this was different. This was an emergency. She'd understand.

Our humanity is based on our ability to choose. In fact, the definition of "humanity" includes the qualities of being humane, of kindness and benevolence, qualities that are not found in the animal kingdom, but only with us humans[24]. We can't be humane without being human, and we aren't human without freewill.

Freewill, however, is not the most important part of this story from Genesis. The real lesson is in the love shown by God when His people failed. Adam and Eve were free to fail, and when they did, God showed them His love. There were consequences for their actions, but they were given with love, equipping them for their life ahead.

Why are we so afraid to admit our failures? Why do we sometimes go to great lengths to "save face," to protect our image in front of others? Sometimes it is out of embarrassment. Sometimes it is out of fear. Someone might reject us if they knew the truth.

This could be true. We might face rejection, but it is in failure that real love can be expressed. The applause we receive for doing well is not as valuable as the

[24]Webster's 1828 Dictionary

love and acceptance given to us by others when we have fallen. Failure gives love the opportunity to be fully expressed.

Is failure the worst thing that can happen in a relationship? No. Distance is. Relationships cannot be worked on, hurt feelings cannot be mended, and misunderstandings cannot be cleared up when people separate from each other. It is only through remaining close to others, even those that have hurt us, that relationships can be more loving, healed, or grow deeper.

Love is a choice, not an assignment. This choice is felt most when it is exercised during times of failure.

This concept of freewill seems like a recipe for producing people that are wounded and hurt, and perhaps it is. How do you put up with, work and live with, let alone love, people who make poor choices?

We do it by first recognizing the part of our humanity that separates us from all other created beings: our freewill. For right or wrong, for better or worse, people get to choose, but because our human nature lends itself to errors in judgment and poor decisions, these choices will not always be good ones. God did not restrict Adam and Eve's ability to choose. Becoming whole begins with knowing that we are all free to make choices and free to fail.

5. Consequences and Compassion

Samantha

Her mom didn't understand.

"Where can she be?" Her emotions were oscillating back and forth from concern to anger and back again. The deadline was clear; Samantha was supposed to be home by 11:30pm and it was now 1:30am. Two hours late. What could she be doing? One thing was certain; Samantha was not going to be able to use the car again anytime soon. She can get her own car and pay for her own gas and insurance from now on.

"I'll ground her for the rest of her life!"

That thought was quickly followed by, "God, please let her be okay."

Choices bring consequences, some good and enjoyable, others more painful. We are all free to make our own decisions, but most of us are also under someone else's authority at least part of the time. We may be under the authority of our parents, our supervisor, the local, state and federal officials, or a commanding officer, but there is almost always someone we answer to. Having to face that person or group of people when we have failed can be both difficult and embarrassing.

Getting caught in their sin appeared devastating for Adam and Eve, so much so that when they heard the sound of God walking in the garden they tried to hide from Him, as if you could hide from God, but they had to do something for their eyes were opened and they had seen the ugly side of their human nature; they had seen their nakedness. Adam and Eve tried to hide their nakedness by sewing fig leaves together, hoping to cover themselves and disappear within the foliage.[25] People still attempt the same thing; only the fig leaves used

---

[25] Gen. 3:7

37

today are in the form of words of justification. If people can justify their actions then maybe their nakedness can remain hidden.

Then the Lord God took the man and put him into the Garden of Eden to cultivate it and keep it. The Lord God commanded the man, saying, "From any tree of the garden you may eat freely: but from the tree of the knowledge of good and evil you shall not eat, for in the day that you eat from it you will surely die.
(Gen. 2: 15-17, NAS)

So Adam and Eve had to suffer the consequences for their actions, but even in the consequences God displays the most amazing part of His nature. The penalty for eating the forbidden fruit was clearly stated: you will surely die. No wonder Adam and Eve hid. They knew what they had done and they knew the penalty for it. They were probably expecting that God would find them and kill them. But God does not kill them. His first words of correction after they sinned must have been shocking, and He wasn't even speaking to them.

The Lord God said to the serpent, "Because you have done this, cursed are you more than all cattle, and more than every beast of the field; On your belly you will go, and dust you will eat all the days of your life; and I will put enmity between you and the woman, and between your seed and her seed; he shall bruise you on the head, and you shall bruise him on the heel. " (Gen. 3: 14-15, NAS)

Eve must have thought she heard wrongly. She may have looked at Adam and asked, "What did He say?" For in the words God speaks to the serpent a message of hope is given to Eve. *"...and I will put enmity between you and the woman, and between your seed and her seed;"* Eve would not die, she would live to produce children, and these children would defeat the serpent. There was hope in the midst of the consequence, and so Eve names her firstborn with that message of hope: Cain, *spear, to strike* (see chapter two). Their nakedness, their frailties and faults were glaringly obvious to them now, but so was the hope. In this moment, with these words spoken to the serpent, God does what He has done for all of us: He extends love and hope.

Love and hope. They weren't struck dead. There were consequences, but there was also hope. This is what separates God from any false god: His expression of love even in the midst of failure and its consequences. God showed His love for His creation the very first time they disobeyed, and gave us a model to strive after in our relationships with each other. The consequences were enacted, but they were enacted with a gracefulness that can teach us how to respond to our own difficult situations.

Samantha pulled the car into the driveway. It was almost 2:30 in the morning now, three hours past her curfew, but it was an emergency. She knew her mom would understand. She was unprepared, however, for her mom's greeting.

"Where have you been? I've been worried sick about you! I didn't know if you were hurt, if you'd been in a wreck, if you'd been kidnapped or what! How dare you come home this late when you knew I'd be up worrying about you!"

Samantha stood there, her mouth open, not knowing what to say.

In every instance of disobedience, of insensitivity, of rebellion and hurt feelings, there is a choice. Can the consequences be administered with hope?

Then the Lord God took the man and put him into the Garden of Eden to cultivate it and keep it. The Lord God commanded the man, saying, "From any tree of the garden you may eat freely; but from the tree of the knowledge of good and evil you shall not eat, for in the day that you eat from it you will surely die."
(Gen. 2: 15-17, NAS)

This is the first and only commandment given to Adam. In it God clearly states the restriction Adam is to follow, and what the consequences will be if he violates it. The Bible does not state, but it is reasonable to assume that Adam communicated this restriction to Eve. They each chose to disobey this commandment, and God must enact the consequences, but in doing so, He extends hope. The consequences are indeed given, but through them He will teach and equip mankind for future life: He will prepare them to be successful even in their failings.

God didn't punish; He followed through. He clearly stated the consequence for eating the fruit of the tree of the knowledge of good and evil, and that consequence was administered. It is easy to think that it would have been more compassionate to omit the consequence all together, to just say, "That's all right. I understand how these things can happen." Real compassion is not about looking the other way or ignoring the problem; real compassion is doing what is best for that person[26]. So, God enacts the consequences.

...for in the day that you eat from it you will surely die.

Did they die? Scripture records that Adam and Eve went on to produce children and to populate the earth. This doesn't sound like a death, but rather a new life. Did Adam and Eve get let off the hook? Where was the death? Where were the consequences?

Consequences occurred in the change of relationship between God and man. Man would have to leave the garden, the special place created just for them, where Adam spoke with God in the cool of the evening.

Consequences occurred in the governorship of the earth. Man was told to subdue and rule the earth, but it had been in a joint partnership with God, with man being able to speak with God and ask Him questions. Man would now have to rule on his own. The decisions he made would be his alone. There was now a distance between man and God.

Consequences also occurred in the loss of man's innocence and purity. Prior to man's sin Adam and Eve only knew God and His holiness, His goodness and purity, and they witnessed it in all of His creation. Now, they knew evil. They were no longer pure. They would no longer see the world through their eyes as God originally created them; now they would see the world through eyes that had experienced and taken part in evil.

Then the Lord God said, "Behold, the man has become like one of Us, knowing good and evil; and now, he might stretch out his hand, and take also from the tree of life, and eat, and live forever,"; therefore the Lord God sent him out from the garden of Eden, to cultivate the ground from which he was taken. So He drove the man out; and at the east of the Garden of Eden He stationed the cherubim and the flaming sword, which turned every direction to guard the way to the tree of life. (Gen. 3: 22-24, NAS)

---

[26] Strong's Hebrew and Greek Dictionaries: H7356 and G4697

Here is the greatest consequence of all, and indeed, the death. God had created a tree of life, and the fruit of this tree was life everlasting. There was no restriction on the fruit of this tree; Adam and Eve had full access to it, and yet they did not choose it. Was it not in season yet? Had the tree not produced its fruit yet and so Adam and Eve would have to wait to eat of it? Did they have to exercise patience for this fruit of life, where none was needed to eat the forbidden fruit? We don't know. The scripture does tell us, however, that the eating of the fruit would cause them to live forever, and that they chose the fruit that would give them the knowledge of good and evil instead. Now, they would die. This remains part of our human condition to this day: we have full access to the source of eternal life, but often choose the knowledge of evil instead.

God's word is true. Like the loving father that He is, He sets the standards and the consequences appropriate to them, consequences that are in accordance with His rules and are best for us as His children.

This is the model for our relationships with each other. There are consequences when we hurt each other, when children disobey their parents and when workers break the rules of their employers, but there are choices within the consequences.

Too often we make this decision based on our emotions. How angry are we? How much did we get hurt? How personal was the infraction? The more personal the hurt, the more it comes from someone close to us, or the more it touches a preexisting hurt or insecurity, the more likely we are to want vengeance instead of justice.

The answer is not found in our feelings toward others or whether or not enacting the consequences makes us uncomfortable or puts us in an awkward situation or even makes us feel better; the answer is found in the other person. What is best for them? What best teaches them, helps them mature and grow, and equips them for the future? What gives them hope?

God was still invested in the lives of Adam and Eve. He cared for them through the consequences of their sin and their betrayal, giving us the model to use in our relationships with each other. Love cares for the guilty. We can care for those who hurt us, who make mistakes that cause us pain and frustration, not because we are soft or weak, not because we are looking the other way and not seeing the problems, but because we are invested in their lives. We can show we care about them. It is in this investment, this decision not to end relationship but to help each other work through the problems, that real love is found. God demonstrated His love to His first family by being true to His word, enacting the consequences, but doing so with hope and continued investment into their lives.

Consequences, as shown by God toward Adam and Eve, are all about showing real love. Consequences should be designed to benefit the guilty, not destroy them.

"Samantha, you know I love you, but what you did was wrong. You are three hours late, you didn't call to let me know what was happening, and you left me to worry about you. You are not allowed to use the car again until we talk through this."

Samantha turned, walked into her bedroom and slammed the door shut.

---

6. Revenge or Justice?

Amy

It wasn't the words themselves that really hurt, although they were mean and unkind, it was that the boss chose to say them in front of the rest of the staff. He had cut her down in front of everyone. She felt belittled and humiliated. And this wasn't the first time it had happened. Amy had spent many sleepless nights replaying situations just like this one, only in her mental replay she had stood up to him, saying just the right things to defend herself and put him in his place. Why was he so mean?

"**!!!## him!" Amy spoke the words to herself. She would never say this aloud, but she said it in her mind over and over again. "Damn him, his family, his business, and everything about him!" She hoped every aspect of his life would disintegrate into a chaos that would leave him completely devastated!

Living and working with people brings conflict. These times of conflict are a certainty of life, just like death and taxes. Some conflicts are relatively minor and can be handled delicately and graciously, while others are more complex, bring more hurts and evoke strong emotional responses. It can be difficult to watch someone get away with something that directly involves us, whether it be a crime, a public embarrassment, or a poorly timed lane change. Some of us respond quickly to these acts of injustice, especially when they seem to be directed at us. If the injustice is not at the level that will involve the local authorities, then we may take action ourselves. The action may involve a physical confrontation, but perhaps most often it is in the form of a spoken, gestured, or at least thought, phrase that is less than kind. There are times, to be sure, that we can rise above these feelings and show genuine love to those with whom we have challenging encounters, and some of us are very good at showing God's love in these situations. There are other times, however, where showing God's love is not only difficult, it isn't even thought of. These challenging situations of conflict can present us with a very difficult question: do we want justice or do we want revenge?

43

Justice and revenge are seen by many as synonymous terms. They both convey connotations of punishment for a wrong committed. Someone who has exacted revenge may be seen as strong, perhaps even heroic. They may be viewed as someone who stood up for themselves and didn't allow others to take advantage of them. There may be truth here. There are certainly times to stand up for our rights and to not allow others to take advantage of us, but the two terms approach these problems from completely different perspectives and purposes.

The Hebrew word for revenge is *"naqam"*[27] and it means the desire for vengeance, a desire to inflict harm on someone else. It does not contain any implication of justice or moral rightness, rather it implies that someone wants to bring harm or damage to another person because of a real or imagined transgression. The purpose of revenge is to exact punishment because we don't want the other person to get away with something. We may think that revenge comes from a sense of justice, from wanting order to be restored, but it is a justice that is self-serving. This is justice as defined by us. We become the judge, jury and executor, if not the executioner. Justice is universal, but revenge is personal.

Justice, on the other hand, is a quality of righteousness. It is a moral principle concerned with the rights and protection of all. The Hebrew word is *"tseh'-dek."* Its uses include a verdict, a judgment, a sentence, or a formal decree. The connotation for this Hebrew word is the justice that belongs only to God. It stems from His goodness and love for his created beings. The charge for those that would enact justice in the Hebrew society was to do so as they believed God would[28].

It is easy to want revenge when we have been wronged, especially if we think the person that wronged us will not be held accountable. This goes against our sense of justice. We want people to be held responsible for their actions. Attempting to interact with those that have hurt us, whether family members, friends, coworkers or casual acquaintances, tests our sense of justice. How do

---

[27] Strong's Hebrew and Greek Dictionary:H5358
[28] Strong's Hebrew and Greek Dictionary: H4941, H6664

we live with and work with, let alone love, these people? Once again, God provides a model for us to emulate.

God was openly defied. His command was not ignored; it was altered by the very beings He had created. These finite beings that were made from the ground and only had life because He breathed it into them, who had everything they needed provided for them by Him, placed themselves above Him in the ultimate act of disrespect. God was wronged. He was sinned against. He could have wanted revenge. We have wanted revenge for a lot less. Instead of revenge God delivered justice.

The LORD God said to the serpent, "Because you have done this, cursed are you more than all cattle, and more than every beast of the field; on your belly you will go, and dust you will eat all the days of your life; and I will put enmity between you and the woman, and between your seed and her seed; he shall bruise you on the head, and you shall bruise him on the heel." To the woman He said, "I will greatly multiply your pain in childbirth, in pain you will bring forth children; yet your desire will be for your husband, and he will rule over you." Then to Adam He said, "Because you have listened to the voice of your wife, and have eaten from the tree about which I commanded you, saying, 'You shall not eat from it'; cursed is the ground because of you; in toil you will eat of it all the days of your life. Both thorns and thistles it shall grow for you; and you will eat the plants of the field; by the sweat of your face you will eat bread, till you return to the ground, because from it you were taken; for you are dust, and to dust you shall return." Gen. 3:14-19, NAS

This sounds a lot like revenge. It is easy to read this portion of scripture and conclude that God exacted vengeance. Adam and Eve broke His commandment so vengeance was sought. God wanted payback and inflicted harm on His people. He cursed them. Or did He?

Look up the word "curse" and you get interesting definitions[29]. It can mean a swearword or profanity, but other definitions include:

- An evil prayer;

---

[29] Webster's 1838 Dictionary

- A malevolent appeal to a supernatural being for harm to come to somebody;

- To wish or pronounce evil on someone.

Is this what God did? Did he pronounce evil on Adam, Eve and their descendants? Do we have pain, suffering and hardship; do we have to work for a living because God cursed us?

No. The scripture in Genesis shows us that God cursed two things: the serpent and the ground.

The LORD God said to the serpent, "Because you have done this, Cursed are you more than all cattle, And more than every beast of the field; On your belly you will go, And dust you will eat all the days of your life; And I will put enmity between you and the woman, And between your seed and her seed; He shall bruise you on the head, And you shall bruise him on the heel. (Gen. 3:14-15, NAS)

The serpent had undermined and twisted God's truth. It attempted to reduce God's words to be something that could be altered by mere human reasoning and experience. With this logic any person could use their own sense of "rightness" to govern and control others by establishing new truths according to their own understanding. God curses the serpent for its arrogance and its attempt to subvert God's plan for His creation, and the curse is severe, perhaps more severe than is commonly believed. God says to the serpent, *"On your belly you will go, and dust you will eat all the days of your life;"* What does this mean? Didn't the serpent already go on its belly, eating dust as it went? This portion of scripture indicates that the serpent was not made the way we currently know it. It is possible that the serpent was originally made with legs and crawled on the ground, otherwise, why would God say, *"On your belly you will go... "*? This illustrates even more strongly the anger God had toward the serpent for its sin. It is possible Adam and Eve saw the legs somehow being removed or falling from the serpent's body as God pronounced His judgment. This must have been a chilling sight.

Then to Adam He said, "Because you have listened to the voice of your wife, and have eaten from the tree about which I commanded you, saying, 'You shall not eat from it'; Cursed is the ground because of you; In toil you will eat of it All the days of your life. (Gen. 3:17, NAS)

God curses the ground, but it is because of Adam's actions, or perhaps, his inaction. God clearly states that the ground is cursed because of what Adam did. *"Because you have listened to the voice of your wife..."* Does this mean that men should never listen to their wives, or that men alone have the power of decision making? No. God is saying that no one, either husband or wife, should ever put their spouse's words above God's. Adam could have not agreed (listened) to his wife and refused to go against God's command. He could have refused to eat the forbidden fruit. Instead, he placed his wife's words above God's.

The first correction given to man established the correct order of relationship. It dealt with how he related to his wife, his helpmate and companion. The first order in God's kingdom is that no relationship should be more important than man's special connection to God. No man or woman can take the place or express the fullness of love and care like God.

The ground was cursed, not Adam and Eve, and not us. What exactly does this mean?

"Curse" is the word most translations use in this portion of scripture. The original Hebrew word is *"ARAR."*[30] It is a primitive root meaning to *"execrate"*[31]: to bitterly curse or to denounce. The strongest connotation, however, is to separate. Prior to this God was joined with man and was a part of his world. God's creative hand was on the earth, and God and man walked the earth together. God's blessing was on His creation and His goodness was in man when He breathed His life into them.[32] Now, because of the sin of Adam and Eve, this would end. When man chose to defy God's direction he himself brought the effects of the curse on the ground. God's protection and creative blessing on His earth stopped with the words: "Cursed is the ground because of you".

Cursed is the ground because of you; in toil you will eat of it all the days of your life. (Gen. 3:17)

---

[30]Strong's Hebrew and Greek Dictionaries: H779

[31]Webster's 1828 Dictionary

[32] Matthew Henry's Commentary Gen 3:1-5

"In toil you will eat of it...." Many interpret this to mean that now, because of Adam's sin, he was made to work for a living; that our having to work is part of the curse, but man was put to work by God before he sinned.

Then the LORD God took the man and put him into the Garden of Eden to cultivate it and keep it. And the LORD God commanded the man, saying, "From any tree of the garden you may eat freely; but from the tree of the knowledge of good and evil you shall not eat, for in the day that you eat from it you shall surely die. (Gen. 2:15-17)

Adam was put in charge of the garden and put to work as an integral part of God's original design. It was part of God's plan that man work. The work we all have to do to earn a living, to obtain the things we need to live, is not a result of sin; it's a part of life. It is part of God's plan.

So what is "toil" referring to? The answer is in the word, "worrisomeness."

This is the word used in the Hebrew text[33]. It translates as sorrow, toil, and pain, and is the same word spoken to both Adam and Eve. This has been translated as "toil," and the words "of it" have been added in modern translations. As is often the case in translating text from one language to another, much of the word's true meaning is lost.

This Hebrew word has no English equivalent. There is no direct translation. It is related to another often-used Hebrew word usually translated as "grieving." It means to "carve out" or "to fashion." It also has connotations of having worry, grief, and anger. Our English translation of "toil" or "pain" appears to be weak, missing the word's true complexities and nuances. "Worrisomeness" seems to be filled with deep emotions including grieving, feeling empathy, and to struggle internally.

The text in Hebrew could read, "Worrisomeness you will eat all the days of your life. No longer will things be simple for you; no longer will the work you do be as easy as it was when we worked together. The full weight of

---

[33] Strong's Hebrew and Greek Dictionaries on Sorrow: H6093

responsibility, concern and compassion for you and your family is now on your shoulders."

Worrisomeness he will eat for the rest of his life. Man would now feel the weight and the responsibility on his shoulders. He would grieve for his loved ones, feel sorry for them, be vexed or angry and hurt by them. Man, who up to this point had only known goodness and purity, would now experience evil, wickedness and cruelty. Now he knew he was capable of engaging with and taking part in evil. Life had now become a lot more complicated. He would experience feelings of sorrow. Emotions of anger and hurt, probably not part of his experience in paradise, would be a part of his life now. He would learn what it means to grieve and feel intense sorrow. These emotions are not part of a curse; they are attributes of God, given to us as we are made in His image. In a way, Adam and Eve had become more like God; they would feel some of the pain He feels when we sin against Him.

God was not gone but was now separated from the earth. Man had chosen to defy the only instructions given. It was not up to God anymore to provide, but for man to seek out what kind of life he would have. God was still there, but could not join Himself with a people that had chosen to blatantly disobey Him. Both of the human beings had chosen defiance. Either one could have put God's standard higher than their personal desire, but they didn't. Their choice had been made.

These are emotions man would live with or "partake of" all the rest of his life, but for the woman it was different.

God then speaks to Eve, and the words spoken to her can appear to be strict punishment until they are also looked into more closely. God is speaking purposely and directly to Eve, saying things to her that are not spoken to her husband.

To the woman He said, "I will greatly multiply your pain in childbirth, in pain you will bring forth children; Yet, your desire will be for your husband, and he will rule over you." (Gen. 3:16, NAS)

If anything sounds like a curse, this does. This verse has been used to explain why the process of childbirth is painful, and that the man is the supreme ruler

49

in the home. A closer look at the original Hebrew gives a different interpretation. Again, we see the same Hebrew word for "worrisomeness."

Unto[H413] the woman[H802] he said,[H559] I will greatly[H7235] multiply[H7235] thy sorrow (worrisomeness)[H6093] and thy conception.[H2032]

Eve's capability for empathy, her ability to feel deeply the hurts and needs of others would be increased. She would feel immense sorrow for others and would toil and work to meet their needs. She would feel pain for others deeply, especially that of her children. She would not be focused only on herself and her own desires and concerns, as she evidently was in the garden. When looking at the forbidden fruit there appeared to be no thought or concern over how her action would affect her husband or her future children. She saw that the fruit was attractive to the eye and good for food, and she ate. Now she would display the characteristics that have embodied women since that time: she would be sensitive and empathetic, she would grieve over their hurts and disappointments. She would be sensitive to the pain and discomfort of others, increasing her ability to care for them. She would have more of God's heart.

"Worrisomeness" is not a curse. It is a gift. It is only because of it we are truly able to care for others. It is only through this strong, often unpleasant emotion, we will care enough to want to mend wounded and broken relationships.

God also told her that He would increase her conception, her ability to produce children (*Unto[H413] the woman[H802] he said,[H559] I will greatly[H7235] multiply[H7235] thy sorrow (worrisomeness)[H6093] and thy conception;[H2032]*). The increase in pregnancies could not be a punishment since having children was their main purpose: to populate the earth. Again, God was increasing something that was already in her, something already blessed and special: her ability to produce children. More was being given to her by God: more ability to produce children in order to fulfill God's plan for their future and more sensitivity to care about it. More worrisomeness. She would feel more, wonder more, and worry more about these special relationships.

The next phrase reads differently in the original Hebrew also: *...in pain you will bring forth children.* The original Hebrew reads: *in an earthen vessel[H6089] thou* *shalt bring forth*[H3205] *children;*[H1121] "Earthen vessel" comes from a word that means to carve out, to fabricate or to fashion[34]. Her children would be hers to raise. She would have to carve out and fashion their upbringing.

The verse could have been written like this: "Unto the woman He said, I will increase your compassion and concerns and your ability to have children. You will labor over them and be responsible for their raising. It will take time, patience and work for you to raise your children. You will be responsible to teach them about love and all the attributes that I have given to you."

God continues to speak to her in a very specific way, but again no curse is spoken.

Yet your desire will be for your husband and he will rule over you. Again, words have been added to the original translation. The Hebrew text reads, *Desire towards husband, he governs*[35]. It does not say "He is the ruler" so bow down and serve his desires in every way. God could be reminding Eve that she was made with the ability to put her focus on many things, children, jobs, friends, the many needs of others, but in doing so to not forget to put her attention on her husband, her partner. God set Adam in position to govern over the earth, and gave him Eve as his co-worker and collaborator.

God did not seek revenge when He was wronged by Adam and Eve, and He doesn't seek it now when we sin against Him. He enacted justice. The differences between justice and revenge begin in the heart and it is the heart that they affect most.

---

[34]Strong's Hebrew and Greek Dictionaries: H6089
[35] Strong's Hebrew and Greek Dictionaries: H4910

51

Justice	Revenge
Brings inner peace.	Brings short-term satisfaction but long-term inner turmoil.
Brings closure.	Brings emptiness.
Serves the greater good.	Is temporarily self-serving.
Is the manifestation of truth.	Is the manifestation of hurt.
Establishes order.	Disregards order.
Benefits all who are involved.	Benefits no one.

We are mandated, as God's people, to rule the earth. Adam and Eve knew this and named their first son accordingly. "Cain," as stated earlier, means "spear," or "to strike." God tells the serpent *"And I will put enmity between you and the woman, And between your seed and her seed; He shall bruise you on the head, And you shall bruise him on the heel.* (Gen. 3:15). Cain's name shows the authority that all mankind would have over the serpent, over evil. We are to rule the earth as stewards of God's creation, and to strike evil, the serpent, when needed.

We are to seek and implement justice, and systems of government have been put in position to help us do just that. We function within our positions of these systems of government, whether they are on the national, state, or local level, or within our position at our job or in the family. We have specific levels of authority based on our positions in these different spheres of influence. We may have a relatively low level of authority in our local community and a much higher one on our job and a higher one yet in our family. Justice is enacted within this sphere of authority. We have the authority to stand up for ourselves; to tell others when something hurts us. This falls under our sphere of influence and authority. We are supposed to care for ourselves, to ensure that we are not being abused or neglected. This keeps us in a healthy state of mind and body, which in turn, puts us in a position to truly care for others.

We cannot, however, require others to conduct themselves in specific ways unless that behavior is specifically related to a level of authority we possess. Even then, we cannot control someone else's behavior. An employer has the right to require a level of behavior from an employee, but the employee has the free will to choose to comply or not. A parent has the right to tell the teenage son what time to be home, but the son still has the choice to obey or to stay out later. Many of our conflicts occur laterally with others that are on the same authority level as us. These people are our friends, spouses and coworkers. We may want to require a certain type of behavior from them, especially if they have hurt us, but we usually don't have the authority to do so. What we can do is love them. We can stand up for ourselves and make our feelings known, and then love them as they make their own decision about their behavior.

Amy walked out of the conference room, still angry. Her boss could be so mean! She didn't really want his world to come crashing down on his head, that was her anger speaking. But she did want him to know how he made her feel. His continued belittling of her in front of others was wrong and it hurt. He was always asking her to take on tasks that were above and beyond her job description, and she always did them. Should she? How could she support this man and his company with extra work and hours when he treated her so poorly? She wanted to be a "team player", she wanted to make the company successful, but shouldn't there be consequences for this man's actions? Amy made up her mind.

Do we want what is best for others, or do we want to pay them back for the hurt they have caused us? Justice will have consequences but these will occur from a sense of moral rightness and a concern for the well-being of all involved.

---

7. Guilt: The Breaker or Builder of Relationships

Amy was angry and hurt. It was cutting through right to the core of her being. She had taken his insults, his public humiliation, his constant degrading long enough. It was time to stand up for herself. With a resolve that blocked her reasoning she walked down the hallway that led to his office. There was no hesitation. There was no rational thought, only cold calculation. Amy had rehearsed this moment in her mind, giving great thought to how this would play out, and now it would. She had chosen her words purposely, selecting the ones that would hurt and humiliate her boss the most, carefully considering which ones would inflict the most pain. That's what this was all about. He had been inflicting pain on her for months. Now it was her turn.

Ted, her boss, welcomed her at the door to his office, smiling and exuding warmth. It was as if he had no clue about her feelings and what he had been doing to her for the last several months. "He knows," Amy thought to herself. He showed her to a seat across from his desk and asked her to sit down.

"Now," he said, "how can I help you?" Amy poised, opened her mouth to speak, and the verbal bile spewed out of her. She lashed out at him, telling him as graphically as possible how he had hurt and abused her. The words were laced with venom, and she could see the shock in Ted's face as they hit him. He was reeling from the onslaught. Amy finished, stood up, turned, and walked quickly, out of the office, waiting for the adrenalin rush of victory to wash over her; but it never came. As she continued down the hall it was a different emotion that surfaced; it wasn't victory or triumph. It was something different. Her "triumphant" act hadn't been completed for 30 seconds and she already knew it was wrong. The feelings of hurt and anger, so strong and powerful just a few moments ago, were replaced with an even stronger one: shame. She passed people in the hallway and felt that everyone was looking at her, as if she were wearing a neon sign that read "Guilty." What had she done?

Guilt. It is perhaps the most powerful of emotions, capable of holding us prisoners and rendering us emotional and social cripples. It can bring pain so powerful that it beats us down with its condemnation, leaving us incapable of either giving or receiving love and compassion.

Why would God give us this emotion? What good can it bring us? The answer can be found in the Garden of Eden, where everything God did was for one purpose.

The first, and perhaps the most important lesson we learn from the book of Genesis is that God is all about relationship. Everything God did, He did for relationship. The creation of the sun, moon, stars, planets, the earth, all living creatures, was all done for the purpose of having loving relationships. God wants a loving relationship with us, and He wants us to have loving relationships with each other.

This phrase gets tossed out almost as an afterthought, or certainly a well-recognized assumption. We would be awestruck, shocked or enthralled to learn that an A-list celebrity or world-class athlete wanted to get to know and hang out with us, but tell anyone that professes to know God that He wants relationship with us and the response you get will probably not be one of amazement, or even mild surprise. On closer inspection, however, this is a mind-blowing fact. The God of all creation, who was and is and always will be, the creator of the universe, wants relationship with you and me.

We are special to God. Three things in the story of creation confirm this.

First, we are created in His image.[36] No other creature, no matter how beautiful, no mountain, no matter how majestic, no star, no matter how spectacular or dazzling, no ocean or planet or any other part of creation can say that. Only us. God created us in His image so that there would be no doubt as to His love for us. We are special indeed.

The story of creation also tells us that we are God's culminating act.[37] After creating the sun and the stars, the earth with its oceans and continents, all the plant life, birds and animals, God created man. Everything else was preparation; and after God created us, He rested. He didn't rest after creating

---

[36] NASB Gen 1:27
[37] NASB Gen 1:26-31

the seas, the plants or the birds. He rested after he created man, after he created us. Even more amazing, however, is the third confirmation of how special we are to God: we are the only part of God's creation that He blessed with the commandment to rule.[38]

And God created man in His own image, in the image of God He created him; male and female He created them. And God blessed them; and God said to them, "Be fruitful and multiply, and fill the earth, and subdue it, and rule over the fish of the sea and over the birds of the sky, and over every living thing that moves on the earth. (Gen. 1:27-28, NAS)

While God did bless the fish of the sea and the birds of the air in Genesis 1:22, this blessing was to be "fruitful and multiply." The blessing given to Adam, and to us, is to rule the earth and subdue it. Man was blessed in his position as God's special creation.

Nothing else in God's creation received this spoken blessing. He looked over the rest of His creative work and said it was good, but He blessed us and gave us dominion over His creation.

Even though we are made in God's image, we are not God, and learning to have healthy, loving relationships with anyone (even God) is not easy for us. God is love, but we are human. Our human nature apart from God's grace is self-centered.[39] It is only through God's grace, which scripture tells us we fall short of,[40] that we are able to overcome our human condition and love each other in a way that reflects God. The natural tendency for all humans is toward self-centered behavior. Loving others in a way that reflects God requires us to learn how God loves and to try to emulate that in our relationships with others. This requires, however, that we put our human tendencies aside and attempt to love as God loves. This attempt lies somewhere between "sort of difficult" and "mind-blowingly impossible" on the difficulty scale depending on the interactions facing us. We are not always successful.

---

[38] Albert Barnes Notes on the Bible
[39] Mark 7: 20-23
[40] Romans 3:23-24

God knows this and is not surprised by it (as we often are). God knows that even though we are made in His image we have to learn how to reflect it. We are often surprised and angered when our relationships with each other don't go as well as we would like. We can be quick to criticize others for their human frailties, especially when they hurt us.

Perhaps nothing is more frustrating than to have to suffer the consequences of someone else's poor decision, unless that poor decision is also accompanied by a seemingly cavalier or even hurtful attitude. We've all been the "victims" of someone's hurtful actions and words, and sometimes we're left scratching our heads at how someone could be so insensitive or uncaring. Why do these people seem to not care that they hurt us? The pain caused by these people increases with the level of closeness we share with them. We can probably get over the pain caused by a complete stranger more quickly than we can by the pain caused by a close friend, family member, or spouse.

We may like to think that in a perfect world people wouldn't behave this way. In a perfect world people would be nice to each other and only do what is right. If all of our needs were met, if we didn't have to strive so hard for what we need and want, then maybe we wouldn't lie and hurt one another. The concept follows the reasoning that if the people had all of their needs met by the government there would be no need for crime, vice, and the other societal ills. History, however, doesn't support the theory. Adam and Eve's first recorded sin didn't occur after they left the garden, when they had to toil and sweat for their daily needs; their first sin, the first sin of mankind, happened in paradise while they were in close relationship with God. They had all they needed and wanted. They lacked for nothing and yet still wanted more. It appears our human nature and its propensity for self-centeredness is not circumstance-specific. This self-serving aspect of our nature can drive us to say and do things we shouldn't, and then to feel the guilt of our inappropriate words or actions.

Guilt. It hurts. It can drive people to run and hide; it can destroy relationships. What a horrible emotion. Or is it?

Guilt is for the emotions what pain is for the body: a signal that something is wrong. We know that something is not right when we suddenly feel pain in some part of our body. We check it out immediately to see what the problem is and what could be causing it. The ability of the body to register pain allows us be aware of small injuries and treat them before they become large ones. The pain we feel tells us that we're doing something harmful to our bodies and we need to change it. Guilt works the same way. It produces feelings that are unpleasant and tells us that something needs to be changed. Our emotions get triggered and send the message that we have done something wrong and need to fix it.

It can be hard to look upon guilt as something good. It is a powerful emotion and most would agree that it does not feel good when we experience it. It is, however, not only positive, it is a gift from God that can be used for our greater good. To not feel guilt is to not feel remorse for hurting someone or breaking a law. It is a vital emotion that enables us to work and live with other people, and it goes hand in hand with another of God's gifts to us described earlier: free will. Webster's dictionary defines guilt this way:

"A state of a moral agent that results from his actual commission of a crime or a sin, knowing it should be a crime or violation of law. To constitute guilt there must be a moral agent enjoying <u>freedom of will</u>, and capable of distinguishing between right and wrong, and a willful violation or intentional violation of a known law, or rule of duty," (Webster, emphasis added).[41]

Our free will, the gift from God that sets us apart from the rest of creation, makes it possible to also feel guilt. We feel guilty when we have freely chosen to do something that ends up getting us in trouble or hurting someone else.

Adam and Eve felt this guilt. As soon as they ate the forbidden fruit this God-given emotion of guilt was felt and they knew what they had done was wrong.

Then the eyes of both of them were opened, and they knew that they were naked; and they sewed fig leaves together and made themselves loin coverings. They heard the sound of the Lord God walking in the garden in the cool of the day, and the man and his wife hid themselves from the presence of the Lord God among the trees of the garden. [(Gen. 3: 7-8)]

---

[41] Webster's 1828 Dictionary on Guilt

Their guilt was telling them that something was not right; they had done something wrong, horribly wrong, and they did what many of us might have done in the same situation, they tried to cover up and hide.

There are two types of guilt[42]. The first one is objective guilt; it is the guilt that we feel because we have truly done something wrong. We are guilty. The child feels this when it disobeys mom and dad. We feel this when we say something out of anger that hurts our spouse or a friend. This is what Adam and Eve were experiencing. They had broken God's rule and they knew it.

The objective guilt they were experiencing could have driven them back to God, running to Him to seek forgiveness for what they had done. Their guilt could have driven them to try to restore their broken relationship with Him. Their guilt was telling them that the situation was all wrong, and that it was their fault, and that they could do something about it, but instead of running to God, running to fix the problem they had created, they hid. They were willing to end their relationship with God rather than fix the problem their guilt had exposed.

The second type of guilt is subjective. We experience the same emotions and feelings, but we haven't done anything wrong. This is the guilt that may be felt when our child gets hurt playing a game and we feel we should have done more to protect them, even though nothing more could have been done. We may feel this guilt when we report someone at work for doing something illegal or immoral and they end up getting reprimanded or even fired. This is the guilt often felt by a child when their parents get divorced or by a wife that is abused by her husband. They feel that it is their fault and things would have been different if only they could have been a better son, daughter or wife. This is not the guilt from God. It is not the guilt given to us that can be used to restore relationships. This subjective guilt is a counterfeit; it devastates people, can leave them emotional cripples and ruin relationships. This guilt needs to be exposed as a lie.

The difficulty with either type of guilt is that it is only directed at ourselves. We can feel anger, hurt, disdain and even bitterness toward others, but we can

---

[42] Oxford Readings in Philosophical Theology, Volume 1, pp. 295-297

only feel guilt toward ourselves. It places us in the position to either admit that we have done something we shouldn't have, or to ignore it, pretend it didn't happen, or perhaps to justify our actions and place blame elsewhere, and to ultimately end relationships.

The objective guilt, the guilt we feel when we truly are guilty, can be the impetus for self-examination, for looking in the mirror critically to see ourselves as we really are, and to make positive changes in our lives. It can drive us toward, rather than away from, those we have hurt or wounded, to work at restoring relationships.

In order to reap the benefits of objective guilt, the guilt we feel when we truly are guilty, we need to respond to it correctly. All too often, however, our response is counterproductive and negates the benefits we could reap. What are our responses to guilt? Reverend Bruce Goettsche of Union Church in LaHarpe, Illinois,[43] provides four responses to guilt that we typically make.

Perhaps the most common response to guilt is to **redirect it**. This is accomplished by either blaming someone else for the problem or rationalizing our behavior. We tell ourselves that this can't really be our fault and someone else must be to blame. Pastor Goettsche provides the following phrases that are all too common to many of us:

- I come from a dysfunctional home; *I'm not responsible; it's my upbringing.*

- This is just the way I am; *it's in my genes, so I can blame evolution or God.*

- They started it; *it's not my fault, it's theirs.*

- I've been oppressed; *it's society's fault.*

Another response to guilt is to **bury it**. If we can put it in a hole deep enough that we can't see it then perhaps we won't have to deal with it. We try to pile the dirt on top of it and smooth it out carefully so that no one will ever know

---

[43] Pastor Bruce Goettshe, Union Church of LaHarpe. Used by permission.

where it is buried. We'll just leave it there and pretend it never existed. This may work for a while, perhaps for an extended time, but even if no one ever finds our buried guilt we will still know it is there. It will continue to affect us until it is dealt with.

If we can't redirect our guilt and we are unable to bury it, then we may try a third option: we may try to **pay for it**. This may be especially true for us in America where it seems that everything is for sale at the right price. Rather than dealing with the reasons for our guilt we may try to buy our way out of it by being extra nice to the other person, or by going out of our way to accommodate their needs or wishes. The spouse dealing with guilt may be a little more considerate or loving than usual. More kind words may be used or more attention may be paid. The price being paid may be valuable and the relationship may go smoother, even better, for a while. Like a cancerous cell, however, the guilt will still be there and will likely surface at some point, perhaps more powerful than it was in the beginning. Attempting to pay for guilt may result in a person that cannot say "no" to the other party. They may spend their lives trying to purchase their way out of their guilt, only to end up frustrated, exhausted and discouraged.

Amy made it to her office quickly, shut the door and sat at her desk. "What have I done?" she asked herself, holding her head in her hands. "This was so wrong. What was I thinking?"

"I shouldn't have said it. I knew it was wrong as soon as the words left my mouth. But I was hurt, and I wanted to hurt him back. I wanted him to know how much I was hurting and I chose the words I thought would inflict the most damage. I did it on purpose, and now the words are out there and I can't bring them back. Oh, how I wish I could! How I wish I could bring them back and no one would remember me saying them. But I can't, and everyone will know what I've done. The irony is; in my attempt to hurt him, I really hurt myself. What do I do now?"

The fourth and the best way of dealing with our guilt is to **confess it**. 1 John 1:9 says, "If we confess our sins He is faithful and righteous to forgive us our sins and to cleanse us from all unrighteousness." The Greek word for "confess" is *homologeo*[44]. It means to publicly acknowledge or proclaim. We cannot confess in private; it is not enough to admit to ourselves that we were wrong and to make a decision to change our behavior. This is good, but it is only the first step. In order to receive the cleansing that God promises we must confess publically. This does not mean we have to stand on the street corner and shout out our transgressions for all to hear. We means we must go to the person or persons involved, admit our wrong doing, and ask for forgiveness. This act of public confession brings cleansing, not only to us but also to the relationship.

"I have no choice," Amy told herself. "There's only one thing I can do. Ted will probably fire me, but then he will probably fire me now anyway. I have to do this. I can't live with this guilt."

Amy stood up, straightened out her clothes and tried to fix her hair and walked out of her office and down the hall. Word of what she had done had already gotten out; she could see it in the faces of her coworkers as she walked by them. She made her way to Ted's office and approached his secretary.

"May I see Ted for a moment?" she asked.

"He's expecting you," was the reply.

We have choices when we are guilty. We can redirect our guilt; we can try to pay for it in some way; we can bury it and hope it goes away; or we can use it to restore broken or wounded relationships. We have the option of confessing our guilt to those we have hurt. They may or may not choose to accept this; that is up to them. We will still be free, however. We will receive the cleansing

---

[44] Strong's Hebrew and Greek Dictionaries: G3670

God promises, and in the process put the relationship in a position to be renewed. We can become whole.

8. Where are you?

Mark

Mark lay on his bed. He could hear his parents' voices downstairs. The fighting seemed to have died down; the voices weren't as loud and there didn't seem to be as much emotion in them. Maybe this would be a good time. Maybe this would help. Their fighting always seemed to be about his dad's job, not having enough money, too many bills to pay. This could be an answer for them. He could help lift some of the burden off of his parents and then maybe they wouldn't fight so much. Mark grabbed the envelope off of his desk and walked downstairs. His parents were sitting in the living room; his dad was watching television and his mom was reading the newspaper. Things were calm now, at least on the outside. He decided to do it.

"Mom, Dad, I have some good news."

They both turned to face him, curiosity on their faces. What possible news could he be bringing them?

He held the letter in his hand and forced a smile.

"I've heard from the university. They've offered me a scholarship. With the money I make over the summer I should be able to go to college in the fall." He put as much excitement into his voice as he could. This really would be good. He could go to college, maybe live on campus and ease the burden for his parents. He wouldn't be in their way all the time. They wouldn't have to spend so much money on food. It would be good that he was gone. Things could be better between them. He did not expect his dad's comment and it hit him hard.

"Why would you want to do that?" his dad asked. There was a touch of frustration in his voice. "College is a waste of time and it's too expensive. You don't need a college degree. Just get a job and start your career now. That's what I did."

"Yeah," his mom said, "and look how well it turned out for him."

"What's that supposed to mean," his dad shot back.

"Maybe if you had gone to college you'd have a real job and we wouldn't be scraping by every month," his mom answered.

That started it again. They were in each other's faces with the words flying everywhere. Mark had tried to help but he just made it worse. He turned and walked back upstairs to his room.

"I can't take this," he said to himself. "I'm not living like this anymore. Everything I do just makes things worse. They think I'm stupid and they hate each other. I'm getting out of here one way or another."

The actions and words of others affect us. The effect may be positive or negative, but we get "jostled" emotionally by what others say and do just as much as when we are bumping shoulders on a crowded sidewalk. Our interactions with others range from the very simple and superficial (the "How are you doing?" we casually throw out as we pass someone on the street) to the very complex. Where these exchanges fall on our emotional meter depends on two things: how important is this relationship to us, and what role does the other person play in our life?

A negative or disapproving word from someone we are not close to or from someone whose opinion we don't value may bump up against our emotions, but can be quickly dismissed, as easily as an inadvertent brush on the shoulder from a stranger on the street. The same words, however, coming from a close friend, spouse or other person whose friendship and opinion we value and covet may leave long-lasting hurts and scars not easily recovered from.

Our human emotions are so sensitive, and our language filled with so many meanings, subtleties and nuances, it is a wonder that we ever really communicate what we actually mean. The potential for miscommunication seems greater than the potential for clarity.

We rarely know all that is happening inside the mind and emotions of others, and because all human interaction is open to misinterpretation the potential for anger and frustration is always close at hand. It may not have taken much for the married couple in this story to have their emotions dissolve into intense anger through a poorly chosen or misunderstood word, phrase or facial expression, but it also may not have taken much for one of them to have expressed regret and shown a desire for reconciliation. The words of anger can come quickly and carry a great deal of impact, but so can the words of love and forgiveness.

How do we respond to the word, phrase or facial expression that appears to have an ulterior motive? Perhaps the intent is not so subtle; perhaps it is overtly angry or condemning. How do we respond then?

God's first question to Adam and Eve is not the question we might ask. Our first question might very well have been, "What have you done?" This is often the first question asked of our children, employees or friends that have wronged us in some way. God's first question is different, and comes from a different motive.

Then the Lord God called to the man, and said to him, "Where are you?" (Gen. 3:9, NAS)

Perhaps no words represent God's love for us better than these. Adam and Eve had sinned against Him, openly defying His commandment, and then ran and tried to hide when they heard Him coming, and yet He still sought them out. He could have easily let them hide in their sin; fester in their guilt, while simply enacting the consequences. After all, they were the ones that had broken relationship, not Him. They were the ones that disobeyed. He had provided everything for them, and this is how they repay Him? Let them come to Him if they want to. Certainly, many of us would have responded this way, and do respond this way at times in our relationships with others. Instead, God sought them out, unwilling to let this sin against Him end their relationship.

This is a question of love, of a Father seeking out His children when they are frightened. The purpose of this question is not to find their location; it is to give them an opportunity. By asking this question God is giving Adam and Eve the chance to come to Him, their loving Father, and admit what they have done; He is calling His children to Him at the time of their greatest need.

Adam and Eve saw their nakedness, perhaps both literally and figuratively. They were most likely physically naked since the time of their creation. There is no evidence that they had worn coverings of any kind up to this point, but it appears from the scripture that now their lack of covering stood out to them.

They were aware, and perhaps ashamed, of their bodies. This shame and embarrassment appears to be directly related to their sin. Their sin had brought about a desire to hide, and this shame now permeated their entire beings. God, in His mercy, provides for them once again, giving them their first clothes.

The Lord God made garments of skin for Adam and his wife, and clothed them.
(Gen. 3:21, NAS)

The love God showed went beyond following through with appropriate consequences. God sees their attempt to cover themselves with leaves and branches, and gives them coverings of skin and fur. God Himself kills an animal, perhaps it was two, and makes garments for Adam and Eve. The clothes God made were not for the purpose of covering their bare skin, but rather they were a tangible expression of covering their mistake. They did not die. Death came to an animal instead; the hide and fur of that animal was used, and their exposed bodies were hidden. This may have been the first time Adam and Eve saw death; a very visual learning experience for this young couple. These new garments were not a sign of their guilt; they were a sign of God's love for them even in the midst of their disobedience.

How blessed is he whose transgression is forgiven, whose sin is covered (Psalm 32:1, NAS)

The Hebrew word used for *forgiven* is *nasa*.[45] It means to raise or lift up, to bear, to carry and to take away. This is what God does for us: He lifts our sins off of us, bears them himself and carries them away. Using the Hebrew definitions the scripture might read this way:

"How blessed is the one whose transgression is lifted off of him to be borne and carried by someone else."

This is what God did for Adam and Eve, and it is what we can do for each other. People will hurt us. They will do things that are unkind and selfish. They will say things that are insensitive and hurtful, and when they do we can do what

---

[45]Strong's Hebrew and Greek Dictionaries: H5375

God does for us: we can forgive them. They may never know what we have done, and they may never change; that is up to them, but we can still care for them the way God cares for us when He asks us, "Where are you?"

Where are you? This question, asked by God in the moment when mankind's relationship with Him was at its most critical junction, shows us how to care for others.

Where are you? This is a question of love. A husband or wife can see their anger quickly defused by this sincere question coming from one that cares for them. It can take time, minutes, hours or years, but whenever someone turns their attention off of their own focus in an attempt to understand the perspective of someone else, love is being expressed.

The act of seeing your mistake and expressing regret is only the beginning for repairing a broken relationship. The other person, the one with the hurt, the one that has felt attacked, also has a choice to make. How do they respond? One response, the one taken many times, is to just agree that the other person was at fault and be finally justified in all the retorts used to point out the injustice.

"You're right, you were wrong. So glad you realized it. Don't let it happen again."

This kind of response, although perhaps accurate, will not go far in helping to heal a hurting relationship. The healing of a relationship, whether it is between friends, coworkers, siblings or spouses, comes not from a desire to be right or vindicated; it comes from a desire to care for someone else. It is seen in the compassion felt for others, even when they have hurt us. It is heard in the question God still asks each of us: Where are you?

This is a perfect example of how to deal with those that hurt us. Instead of choosing to stay in our hurt, hoping the other party is feeling it worse than we are, we can be unwilling to let the hurtful incident end the relationship. We can follow God's example. We may be able to go to them, seek them out and find ways to care for them. We may even be able to forgive them.

68

Mark put down his pencil and looked at the letter he had just written. It expressed all of the emotions he had kept bottled up. It told his parents in no uncertain terms how much their constant fighting hurt him, how he couldn't take it anymore and that he was moving out as soon as he could. He read it again, looking to see if he used the perfect words, the ones that would inflict hurt and wound his parents the way they wounded him. He felt completely justified in this decision.

His eyes, still looking at his letter of vindication, caught the image of his scholarship notice from the university. He turned his focus to it, wondering why this letter of good news had made things worse. He opened it and read it again.

"We are pleased to inform you..." it began. Such good news. Such validation of him and his future. This university wanted him. He had potential. He could make something of his life.

Then it struck. This was all about him. Everything he was feeling was focused on himself. It was about his feelings, his anger, his frustration, his scholarship. What about his parents? What were they feeling? They couldn't like living like this; why did they? How much hurt were they feeling? How much pain, frustration and anger? He couldn't live like this, but he couldn't leave, either. He loved his parents too much. He had to talk to them. He had to tell them how he felt, his anger, his frustration, but also his love for them. He had to give them the opportunity to listen to him and respond if they chose to. He picked up the letter he had written, crumpled it up, threw it into the wastebasket, and then walked downstairs.

"Mom, Dad, can we talk?"

9. Where Am I?

Samantha sat on her bed. She hadn't come out of her room since she got home late last night and it was now late Saturday afternoon. "My mom is out of it!" she thought to herself. "She doesn't understand me and is completely out of touch with the things I have to deal with!"

She needed to talk to someone, but she wasn't about to go talk to her mom, so she got out her phone and texted Janet, the girl she was trying to help the night before.

Samantha: my moms tckd. i'm grnded 4 life. she wont EVR let me use the car again ☹

Janet: you can lve w me ☺

Samantha: i might as well   cant seem to plse my mom

Janet: lets do it ☺ ☺ *my mom wont care. she's not around*

Samantha: maybe, my moms drivng me insane

Janet: lol :-}

Samantha heard her bedroom door open and quickly tried to put her phone under the pillow.

"Samantha, we need to talk," her mom said as she stood in the doorway.

"I can't talk now. I've got too much homework to do," was Samantha's curt reply.

"It doesn't look like you're doing homework now. It looks like you're texting on your phone."

"Does it really matter what I do? Nothing I do seems to please you anyway. Even when I try to help someone I get in trouble!"

Perspective is everything. It provides our frame of reference for every situation we ever encounter, and it is out of this frame of reference that we formulate our actions and the words that will explain or justify them. Everything we do is based on how we view the facts, and we view the facts through a measured assessment of what we see before us. This perspective, this lens through which we see the world, this schema as described earlier, has two critical components: it is personal and it is present tense.

It is personal because it is unique to us. It is formed out of every encounter, every interaction we have ever had. It is influenced by the books we've read, the movies we've seen, the experiences we've had, and where and how we grew up. Everything in our lives helps construct our perspective on life, and because we are unique individuals, with unique personalities, qualities and experiences, our perspectives are unique. Even identical twins, with identical DNA, growing up in the same home, will have unique perspectives based on their unique interactions with parents, siblings and friends.[46]

It is present tense because it is ever-evolving. We have new experiences daily. We meet and interact with new people every day. We see the world differently today than we did a few years, months, or even days ago because we have had new experiences that have helped shape and reshape our perspective.

We can only respond to the situations of life out of our personal perspective, out of our schema. The problem is our perspective is limited; we can only see through the lens of our life. It is akin to seeing only part of a photograph, being limited by its boarders and frames. We can say and do things that seem appropriate from this limited viewpoint, only to regret them later when we may see a much bigger picture.

When God asked Adam and Eve "Where are you?" their perspective was His primary focus. It was an opportunity for them to look at their guilt and expose their own view and understanding of their situation. This is the most loving and caring position we can take. Instead of evaluating and making judgments on others, we can let people evaluate their emotions and motives for

---

[46] Piaget, 1954

themselves. It is the only way we can ever know the thoughts, views and concepts in the minds of others. That is what God did for Adam and Eve and it provides the beginning of the question we can be asking ourselves all the time.

"Where am I?"

It can be a difficult question. It's impossible to arrive at the answer without honest examination, a willingness to stand in front of our emotional mirror and see the unsavory things that are kept hidden by our nice clothing. The problem with the mirror is that it doesn't lie. It doesn't even politely exaggerate. It shows exactly what is there, whether we like it or not.

Self-examination is not easy. We all want to look good in front of others, and the one person we most want to look good in front of is our self. Self-examination could lead to the one conclusion we most dread: we are guilty. It is one thing to have someone else think we've done something wrong; we can dismiss their verdict with a variety of justifications that most of us have used at some point in time: they don't have enough information; they're misinformed; they weren't there so they don't know; or, who are they to judge me? But when we examine ourselves, truthfully and honestly, these justifications no longer work.

The answers I face as I look into my emotional and mental mirror can either be liberating or incarcerating. It can be liberating and I can feel the freedom that comes with knowing that I have conducted myself with honesty, maturity, and concern for others. I can recognize that I have tried to treat others the way I want to be treated, and I have made amends when I have fallen short. I have made mistakes; I've said and done things that were insensitive and perhaps even hurtful, but I have owned these mistakes and worked to have caring relationships with others. I see the blemishes in my reflection in the mirror, but that's okay; I'm working on them.

Or, I can feel imprisoned by my selfish acts or my lack of care and concern for someone else. I have been hurt and allowed this hurt to compel me to anger, anger I've actually enjoyed and nurtured. I've focused on myself and not cared for others. I spoke cruelly to someone and didn't care enough to make it right. I feel the guilt of these things and I'm held under its lock and key.

Guilt, as discussed earlier, is a powerful emotion given to us by God to tell us that we have done something wrong and need to fix it. It can be the incentive for us to admit our wrongs and restore our relationships. When not heeded, however, when guilt is allowed to take root in our emotions it grows like a cancerous cell and becomes something that is not from God, something that can completely immobilize us and thwart our emotional growth and render us relational cripples. It becomes shame.

Stephen Pattison is the author of the book, <u>Shame: theory, therapy and theology</u>.[47] In it he describes two different types of shame. *Acute reactive shame* is similar to objective guilt and results from knowing and accepting that we have done something wrong. We are shamed by our actions, and, as in the case of objective guilt, we can use this feeling to admit what we have done and to right the wrong. This shame is painful, but if dealt with can be temporary.

The other type of shame is *chronic shame*. This shame often results from extended exposure to guilt, whether objective or subjective, and "...can cast a permanent shadow over a person's life, character and personality." [(Pattison, p. 83)]

Not dealing with our objective guilt, the guilt we feel because we are indeed guilty, plants the seed of chronic shame and it is watered and fed over time by the unresolved guilt we fail to deal with. This is the shame that leaves us immobile, paralyzed by the weight of our wrongdoings. And this is the shame that ruins our relationship with God, and our relationships with each other.

Both types of shame must be dealt with to have healthy relationships.

To You, O Lord, I lift up my soul. O my God, in You I trust, Do not let me be ashamed; Do not let my enemies exult over me. Indeed, none of those who wait for You will be ashamed; Those who deal treacherously without cause will be ashamed. [(Psalm 25: 1-3, NAS)]

In this prayer for guidance and protection King David demonstrates the power of shame, but the original Hebrew word brings even more light to his petition.

---

[47] Stephan Pattison, 2000

The word for "ashamed" in this scripture is *buwsh*.[48] It means to feel ashamed or disgraced, but it also means something else: to pale. We are made in God's image. The word for "man" is *Adam* and one of its meanings is "to show blood."[49] We are the only animal created by God that shows blood through our skin. All humans, regardless of race, show their blood; it is seen in the veins in our arms and legs, in the blush in our cheeks, and over our bodies that are unique to our species and not covered by fur. Red is the color of life, the color of the blood that every cell in our body must have to survive, and when we are ashamed we lose this color. We pale. The reddish color that we all have leaves us; our faces become ashen. Pale is the color of sickness, a sign that our blood is not flowing as it should.

When we "pale," when we are ashamed, we lose our vibrancy, our vitality. We no longer reflect God's image in its fullness, His life and effervescence. This is what unresolved guilt does to us. It brings us to shame, taking us further away from who God made us to be. King David recognized that his trust in God was the source of his vitality; it was the source of life for his soul, and without it he would pale and be sickly.

The hold of chronic shame can be broken. We can return to a state of vibrancy and life, personally and in our relationships. The rich hue of God's life running through us can be restored.

The thief comes only to steal and kill and destroy; I came that they may have life, and have it abundantly. (John 10:10 NAS)

God's plan for us is to have an abundant life, one that is extraordinary, excellent, beyond what we can think or ask,[50] a life that is rich, like the blood that he gave us when He breathed into Adam. This blood is filled with the fullness of love and compassion. It is the substance of life itself.

We often play the "Rank My Sin" game. We look at our faults and compare them to others to see how we measure up. Of course, our comparisons are with those that we know are much "worse" than we are; it wouldn't be any fun

---

[48] Strong's Hebrew and Greek Dictionaries: H954
[49] Strong's Hebrew and Greek Dictionaries: H120, H119
[50] Ephesians 3:20

to compare ourselves with someone whose faults are less than our own. So, we end up making comparisons like these: "I haven't robbed any banks today. I haven't sold drugs on the street today; I haven't killed anyone lately, so I must be doing okay."

These statements are probably (hopefully) true, but they are self-selected to photograph us in the best light possible. The truth is that we all make mistakes and that many of our mistakes hurt other people. It is all about perspective.

Thirty minutes later Samantha was still sitting on her bed. She hadn't moved or spoken since her mom had come in asking to talk with her. She just sat there in silence. Her anger, having been simmering on her emotional burner for some time now, was near the boiling point. What was her mom's problem?

"Janet needed my help!" She thought to herself. "She was in no position to drive! I may have saved her life! Mom has no right to be mad at me!"

It was not easy to be angry toward her mom. She and her mom had been close her whole life. While her friends were in constant conflict with their moms, Samantha and her mom were always close, doing things together and talking together. It hurt there was now a separation between them.

Samantha lay down. This was so wrong. Her head hurt; her stomach hurt; her whole body ached. Why was she feeling like this? Was her mom right? Is that possible? Was she wrong? Should she have made sure to call home first? It seemed like the right decision at the time. What if she was wrong? What if her mom was right?

She stood up and walked toward the door.

We can't change others, but we can change ourselves, and self-examination using God's love as our standard of measure is the agent of that change. God can ask the questions, but He leaves the power and responsibility to change up to us. No one can do this for us. People can give us great information, they can give us their opinions and viewpoints, but only we can decide to make changes in our life. We get to decide if and how to measure truth against our actions. Our perspective is just that, ours, and it won't change until we allow it.

Perspective changes everything.

10. The Gift

Steve

He had been a good husband, hadn't he? He provided her with a good home and all the comforts she could want. There was money for trips, new clothes and a nice car. What more did she want from him? He was not to blame here!

He picked up the paper with the horrible words blaring on it. He folded it up and tucked it away in his desk. His kids would be home from school soon. It would take time to figure out how he could respond to her "request." He really had no idea what should be done next, except he didn't feel justified anymore or vilified. He just felt accepted by God's love. That was one thing he knew about and could trust in. He knew there were things he had done that were not the most loving towards his wife over the years. Maybe there were things he could do to help change her mind about ending their marriage commitment, maybe not. What could he do to show his love to her?

What can a person do when they find themselves in a position of hopelessness? How do we navigate through life's sea of despondency, a foreboding body of water that can seem impassable, and one that we often find ourselves in because of our actions and/or the actions of others? Why are the faults and problems of others so obvious to us and so oblivious to them? We see the life-changes that others need to make and we can want so desperately for these to happen; and yet we cannot make them happen. We cannot change others. In truth, we can have a very difficult time changing our own behavior and life patterns, and while the faults of others often stand out to us as if they are written in neon signs, our own faults, which may be larger still, can go completely unnoticed.

But change can happen. We are not sentenced to a life of poor decisions, unfulfilled relationships and interpersonal conflicts. These may crop up in our life from time to time, but they do not have to be the norm by which our life is lived.

We can see our blemishes and warts, our sin, and we can do something about them. We can change.

Loving others is not always easy, and at times it is very difficult. Our human nature and our unique personalities are filled with very individual likes, dislikes, idiosyncrasies, personal habits, quirks and mannerisms. Some of these are sort of cute, others are just plain annoying, and some are wrong and need to be eradicated completely. Add to these personality traits the complications of life and its many obstacles and pitfalls and it can be a wonder that we get along with each other at all. The first family, after the failure in the Garden, didn't have it any easier, and it was during this time that the two boys decide to take action, and this action changed everything.

So it came about in the course of time that Cain brought an offering to the Lord of the fruit of the ground. Abel, on his part also brought of the firstlings of his flock and of their fat portions. And the Lord had regard for Abel and for his offering. (Gen. 4: 3-4, NAS)

Cain decides to bring a gift to God, and this scripture indicates that he had the idea first, before Abel. Why? Why did Cain, and then Abel, want to bring gifts to God? Was it an attempt to appease God, to get back in His good graces? Was it to try to get back into the Garden of Eden, or was it just to show their love for God? We don't know. Whatever the reason, both sons decide to bring a gift, and they chose their gifts from the jobs they performed for the family. Cain was the tiller of the ground, the farmer and the orchardist. His gift would be the fruits and vegetables that he raised. Abel was the shepherd. His gift would be entirely different, and it doesn't sound all that appealing. Abel's gift was the "fat portions" of his flock.

What kind of a gift to God are the fat portions of a bunch of animals? How did he come up with this? Cain's idea of fresh, ripe, succulent fruits and vegetables as a gift certainly presents a nicer image than that of the inner parts of a sheep. And what exactly are "fat portions" anyway? And it was Abel's gift, this gift of the inner parts of an animal that was accepted by God! What was behind this gift? What was its significance?

Abel's gift was probably two kidneys surrounded by fat. The scripture in Genesis 4 doesn't state this directly, but the sacrifices outlined later in the Bible describe it in great detail.

"You shall take all the fat that covers the entrails and the lobe of the liver, and the two kidneys and the fat that is on them, and offer them up in smoke on the altar." (Ex. 29:13, NAS)

These are the directions given to Moses from God on how the people are to offer their sacrifices to Him. It is reasonable to believe that they follow the first accepted gift offered by Abel, and these instructions match the wording of "fat portions."

Kidneys and fat! How do these two things represent an acceptable gift to God? An examination of their significance in our body's ongoing fight for survival may help. Blood is the source of physical life. It gives us color and richness. Because of our blood we are not pale but rich, alive and vibrant. It provides strength and protection. Understanding the biology of blood and kidneys gives us a clear picture of why this gift was so special.

The red blood cells are the distributors in our bodies. Each cell in our body is in close proximity to a blood capillary, and it is here in the capillaries that red blood cells do their work. They are like little wagons that travel throughout our bodies, bringing oxygen and nutrients to every cell. Each cell is in constant need of replenishment to do its work and it is the job of the red blood cells to deliver it. These same blood cells are also the garbage men of the body. After they have delivered their precious cargo of oxygen and nutrients, they gather up the waste lest poisonous by-products pile up and cause harm. Through a chemical process of gas diffusion and transfer, individual red blood cells in the capillaries absorb waste products from these cells. The red cells then deliver these waste chemicals to organs that can excrete them from the body.[51]

The primary organs of excretion are the kidneys. Excretion is vital to the health of the body because the wastes it incurs are poisonous. If the wastes build up and are not eliminated they can cause serious health problems. Urea,

---

[51] In His Image, pp. 75-80

various salts and other waste products are taken through the blood stream where they are removed by the kidneys. The blood is stripped of such components causing them to be separated for disposal and only usable products are kept and returned into the blood stream. 42 liters of water are filtered and returned to the body each day, causing one or two quarts to be eliminated. This keeps the toxic products diluted, unable to cause damage to tissues as they pass from the body. This process of washing the blood of its impurities happens at least 36 times a day.[52]

Washing and cleansing. 36 times a day. Perhaps nothing paints a clearer picture of us as humans and our status before God. We need to be washed and cleansed daily. How often? How often do we have thoughts that are contrary to the purposes of God? How often do we exhibit impatience or anger toward others? How often are we quick to judge others while wanting only mercy for ourselves? How often do we feel trapped in hopelessness? How often are we human?

The design of our human bodies is a perfect example of us, our relationship with God and our relationships with each other.

Our bodies are not designed to function only when things are operating perfectly; they are designed by God to be able to deal with the problems they encounter daily through the course of everyday living. Every day, through the normal process of life, our bodies are subject to things that are not good for it, and if left alone, could cause major health problems. Everything we eat, no matter how many healthy things they may have in them, also contains waste products that must be eliminated from our bodies for us to remain healthy. The normal amount of food taken in during the course of a typical day would pose a serious health threat if the body were not able to break it down for use and disposal. God designed our bodies with a process in place to handle the variety of foods and liquids we take in.

God designed our emotions in the same way. We do not live in a perfect world where our emotions are only fed things that are nurturing and supportive. Our world includes hundreds of interactions every week, and not all of them are

[52] Encyclopedia of Human Biology, vol. 3, pp 94-95

pleasant or easy. Some make our life difficult and some bring emotional hurts. Just like the cells in our bodies, our emotions and our minds need to be restored, and just like the millions of cells that make up our bodies, each one never more than a hair's breadth away from a capillary, we need to be in close contact with God. When this happens, our emotional and mental beings have the capacity to recover. Just as the body is designed with mechanisms for cleansing and purifying, our emotions, our mind and our spirit can also be cleansed. The kidneys are the cleansing agent for the body, and God is the cleansing agent for our emotions. The hurts we receive through the words and actions of others, as well as the guilt we feel when we are the inflictor of these hurts, can be absorbed and removed through our relationship with God. This is done through forgiveness and repentance.

Forgiveness is not always easy. We want justice when we feel we've been wronged, and to forgive someone can feel as if we are letting them off the hook. They get away with it. Forgiveness is not looking the other way as if nothing ever happened; it is looking into the heart of the other person and seeing what is best for them. Enacting consequences for someone's actions may not only be appropriate, it may be helpful, perhaps even merciful. Appropriate consequences can teach us about responsibility, about maturity, and about how to treat others. God enacted consequences for Adam and Eve, as He does for us today, but, as stated earlier, He does this with our best interests at heart.

"Repentance" is not a commonly used word in our American culture. It can be seen as a sign of weakness, and is not correctly modeled for us in most instances. The "repentance" we see in many, if not most, cases is not true repentance at all. It often sounds something like this: "I'm sorry if my (words, actions) offended anyone."

The word "if" qualifies the statement and places the weight of responsibility on someone else. It is analogous to saying, "My words should not have offended you, but if they did then my saying 'I'm sorry' should take care of it and we can move on."

Webster's dictionary defines "repentance" this way: to feel pain, sorrow or regret for something done or spoken; to express sorrow for something past; to change the mind in consequence of the inconvenience or injuries done by past conduct.[53]

We feel the pain of what we have done or said. It brings us shame and sorrow and we want to fix it.

True repentance does not say, "I'm sorry if...", it says "I'm sorry for..."

We take ownership of what we have said or done. It is a changing of our mind, of how we think. We have a schema for right and wrong just as we have a schema for everything else. It is possible that we do not view our actions as hurtful. We may not perceive what we have said or done as being harmful and we may view the other party as weak or too sensitive for being offended. Our way of relating, our jokes, even our physical interactions may seem friendly, perhaps even endearing to us. We may think they are cute and lovable, while others may perceive them to be childish, boorish or even bullying.

This repentance requires that we 1) are willing to examine our schema for appropriate behavior to see if it is truly accurate, 2) are willing to look into our emotional and mental mirrors and be willing to see the truth reflected in the image, and 3) have the strength of character to humble ourselves, to care enough about the other person involved, to go to them and admit what we have done.

This repentance breaks the yoke of shame and leads to the restoration of relationships.

By faith Abel offered to God a better sacrifice than Cain... Heb. 11:4

The writer of Hebrews says that Abel's sacrifice was offered by faith. This is a man whose very name means "vanity" or "worthless." What was the source of his faith? Faith in what? It couldn't have been faith in himself. Perhaps it was faith in God's ability to cleanse him when he could not do it himself. Abel must have recognized his frailty, his weakness and propensity to sin, perhaps through his name, the coverings he had to wear or the interactions with his

---

[53] Webster's 1828 Dictionary

family. In all of these he may have seen that God was the only answer to his problems. He needed cleansing. The only way to be reconciled with God when we have failed to represent His holiness is to express our desire for cleansing and change. Seeing our human condition clearly, as it compares to God and His holiness, provides us with a clear understanding of our position in relation to God. Abel's gift of kidneys is a perfect example of our human condition and our need for God. It provides the perspective necessary to come before God for cleansing and healing.

Abel's life changed. He is no longer remembered as vain and insignificant. Abel is now known as faithful and righteous. Abel's name, once denoting vanity and emptiness, now gives us insight into our natural tendencies, and our ability to change and grow beyond them. Our lives can be seen and remembered in a way that reflects God.

Our job is to take responsibility over our own lives by facing our guilt, seeking forgiveness and taking the necessary steps to restore broken relationship with God and others. This is the way we can truly change. This is the way we become whole. This is an expression of love and life. Renewal, restoring, and reconciliation. These are the words of relationship.

"Good morning," Steve said as he walked up to her and hugged her, interrupting her cooking in the process.

"Good morning to you," she answered, allowing her routine to be interrupted once again. It seemed like he was always interrupting her, changing her plans, coming up with spontaneous ideas that took them to who-knows-where. It was one of the things she loved about him, but it hadn't always been that way. She loved her routines and her order. They gave her direction and focus, things she valued highly, but Steve wasn't like her. He liked surprise and change. He was energized by creativity and spontaneity.

She found this amusing early in their relationship, but only slightly so. She figured that he would "grow up" after they married. In truth, she had tried to change him, to make him more like her, but it didn't work. "Changing him" turned into controlling him, and their relationship had suffered.

She hugged him back, happy to have this creative and imaginative man for her life partner, and returned to making breakfast.

The Gift

Steve poured himself some coffee, sat at the table and marveled at how fortunate he was. This table, this very same table was where he found the note 20 years ago. He remembered the anger he felt back then, and he remembered blaming his wife for being so critical of everything he did, of being so controlling. He remembered the hopelessness; but it wasn't hopeless. He could have remained mired in his anger, blaming her for all the bad things in the marriage and exalted himself for all the good. But he knew better. It couldn't be that simple. So he made a decision. He began to examine, really examine his life. He asked for help from a close friend, one he knew would care about him enough to be honest. What he heard wasn't pretty. All the fun, spontaneous, even gregarious parts of his personality, the very things Steve prided himself on, became annoying after a while. It wasn't that these personality traits were bad; on the contrary, they were part of who he was and made him fun to be around. They also became obnoxious when overdone, and Steve knew he overdid them a lot. He had to admit that many times he focused on himself, trying to be the "life of the party," evidently at the expense of others. Steve then went to talk to his wife.

She told him the same thing; that his "carefree" attitude, his penchant for wanting to go wherever his emotions took him, had crossed the line from being "fun and exciting" to being "childish and irresponsible." It was true that she constantly told him how to do things and even what to do, but part of that was because he made her feel that he wouldn't do anything otherwise. His "free-spirited thinking" was seen by her as indecisiveness and instability. It brought her feelings of uncertainty; of feeling she needed to take charge because she didn't think he would, of thinking she might be better off without him.

So he had gone to her and repented, openly admitted his faults and asked for forgiveness. He didn't beg for her to come back, that was her decision, but he took ownership of his faults and took the first step to making real life changes. That act of honesty and humility opened the door for them to talk openly and to begin to work on things. They both learned to truly listen to each other and repent and forgive when needed. Now here they were, 20 years later, still married and more in love than ever. They found ways to work together, his creativity and spontaneity meshing with her focus and order. The result; they were both freer to be who they were, their natural gifts and ways of thinking enhanced by those of their partner. They were better together than they ever would have been apart.

Steve still had the note. He kept it as a reminder of what almost happened; of how his life was almost ruined and of how much better his life was now.

11. The Sweet Smell of Reconciliation

Amy

Amy knocked on the door and Ted opened it, not looking so warm and inviting this time. Amy gathered her resolve, looked him in the eye and said, "Ted, there is no excuse for what I just did. I was wrong. Please forgive me."

Ted looked hard at Amy as they stood facing each other in his office. Just a few minutes before she had left his office after unleashing what could only be described as a verbal attack. Abhorrent words had poured out of her mouth, accusing him of being disrespectful, uncaring, insensitive and worse. Now she stood before him with an apology, like that would erase all that had happened. Ted continued to look at her; not speaking. If he had learned anything in his years of being a manager of people it was to not speak when he was angry. He forced himself to remain calm, gestured to a chair, and said, "Why don't you have a seat and tell me what you are feeling."

We are complex beings, physically and emotionally, and this complexity makes interpersonal relationships complicated and problematic. We say and do things through lapses in judgment, through anger and selfishness, and sometimes out of spite and wanting revenge. The closer the relationship, the more our lives are intertwined with another person, the greater the opportunity for hurt feelings. Close relationships can produce the greatest joy, fulfillment and love, but they can also bring the greatest hurt.

We are born with the capacity to love others, but we are also born with a predisposition for self-centeredness. It takes work to reconcile these two areas of our lives. Love for others is the cornerstone for successful relationships and relating successfully with others is the essence of a whole, fulfilled life. We must learn how to love, and we learn this best in our relationships with others.

Abel's gift to God was an act of restoration. He was reaching out to God, knowing his weaknesses and frailties but willing to come to his God in humility. It was an act of relationship.

And thou shalt take[H3947 (H853)] *all*[H3605] *the fat*[H2459] *that covereth*[H3680 (H853)] *the inwards,*[H7130] *and the caul*[H3508] *that is above*[H5921] *the liver,*[H3516] *and the two*[H8147] *kidneys,*[H3629] *and the fat*[H2459] *that*[H834] *is upon*[H5921] *them, and burn*[H6999] *them upon the altar.*[H4196]

Abel's gift of kidneys surrounded by fat provides a perfect example of a close relationship. This was not just any fat in the body, of which there seems to be no shortage, the fat described in this portion of the bible was perirenal fascia[54], the fat that is above the liver and surrounds the kidneys. It was not the stomach fat from too much food. It was not the fat that puts a layer underneath our skin, but the fat that clings and protects this very important organ of cleansing. This fat clings so closely to the kidney, covering and protecting it, that it cannot easily be removed. This fat sits above and behind the abdominal cavity that is above the liver. Like a husband and wife or two close friends these two bodily members are not easily separated. A sharp knife has to be used to cut the fat away from the kidney. They are constant companions, joined in a common function and inseparable except by force. Separate one from the other and they are less efficient. Just like people, they are designed to function together.

It is only in relationship with others that we can become whole people, the people we are designed to be. Shortly after creating Adam, the first man, God declared that it was not good that there was only one of him. It was not good that he was alone.[55] We are not designed to be alone, and as much as we value our independence, as much as we like to think of ourselves as strong and self-sufficient, we need other people. We're created that way.

It is through relationship with others that we learn, about ourselves, about others, and indeed, about life. Lev Vygotsky, a Russian medical doctor, psychologist and educator, said that learning is a social act, that all real learning is a product of communication with others.[56] There is no shortage of educational research that points to relationships as a key ingredient in teaching others. Noted educator and literacy expert Regie Routman states that the first

---

[54] Gray's Anatomy, pp. 1114, 1270
[55] Gen. 2:18
[56] Vygotsky, 1978

job of a classroom teacher is to bond (make relationships) with his/her students.[57]

All of this points to our need for relationships in almost every area of our lives. We especially need relationships to make any lasting change.

Sitting across from her boss was different this time. Amy didn't feel confident, angry, spiteful, or any of the other emotions that had been so prevalent just a short time ago. She was ashamed. The only way to resolve this was to come clean, to tell him everything.

"I'm hurt by the way you treat me in front of the others. I feel put down, demeaned, ridiculed and made fun of. Instead of speaking with you honestly about these feelings, I let them grow into anger and then I lashed out at you. Again, this does not excuse my actions. I was wrong. I treated you disrespectfully and I'm sorry. I should have respected you enough to speak with you truthfully."

Ted listened, still angry but also concerned. This is how she felt? These were just jokes. They were meant to lighten up the workplace and to inject some fun into their meetings. She took these seriously? He wondered if others took them seriously, too. Was this the kind of boss he was? Did he need to change?

Why should I change? What does it matter? Whom will it affect? If I have no real relationships with other people then there is no good answer to these questions. Why bother to change if I'm not in relationship with someone? Any relationship I may have is superficial, and I can fake my way through those. Taking this a step further, if we have no real relationships with other people, then it is likely that we won't even know we need to change. It is through relationships with others, close, caring, relationships, that we truly learn of the areas of our lives that need changing and gain a desire to deal with them. Many people are willing to tell you your faults. They may be only too glad to

---

[57] Routman, 2003

point out all of your shortcomings, but a true friend, a loved family member or spouse, will have a different motive. They want what is best for you, to see you be successful in life and in relationships, and are willing to risk potential anger and hurt to help you get there.

Do we want to change? Do we think we really have to? Do we think it is even possible? I've heard people say that they cannot change, and often the same two reasons are given:

- I'm too old to change.

- I'm just made this way.

The problem with these is that they don't hold up with science or scripture.

Science classifies objects for the purpose of studying and understanding them. The first classification consists of two categories: living or nonliving. One of the criteria for something to be classified as "living" is that it has to grow and change.[58] The Oxford dictionary states that life is "...the condition that distinguishes animals and plants from inorganic matter, including the capacity for growth, reproduction, functional activity, and continual change preceding death..." To be alive is to change continually. This happens throughout the entirety of the life cycle. None of us look now the way we looked as infants. There may be some similar characteristics, but we have all changed, so much so that someone might not be able to pick our baby picture out of a group. Those of us that are older, say 50s or 60s, do not look the way we did in our 20s. We also do not think in the same ways, barring some horrible emotional crisis that abated our maturational process. The thinking processes we employed as an infant were different than that of our adolescence, different than that of our young adult hood, and different than that of our senior years.

Scripture also points to our ability and need to change.

When I was a child, I used to speak like a child, think like a child, reason like a child; when I became a man, I did away with childish things. (1 Cor. 13:11, NAS)

---

[58] Oxford Dictionaries.com/Webster's Dictionary

This scripture tells us that our ways of thinking grow and mature, and that they change over time. We are never too old to learn more of God's ways.

The second reason, "I'm just made this way," represents a misunderstanding of what it means to change. God made us unique individuals, with very specific and tailor-made characteristics. There is no need to change how God made you. Perhaps He made you very orderly and administrative. Good. Perhaps he made you very lively, with the ability to make people laugh. What a wonderful gift. Perhaps he made you very meticulous, with the ability to see all sides of an issue or problem and to seek out solutions. Perfect. These are God-given traits that He gave you to use and develop. We have also picked up a lot of characteristics from the influences of the world around us that are not Godly, and these influences can render our God-given talents ineffective at best, and hurtful at worst. Our ability to see all sides of a problem, 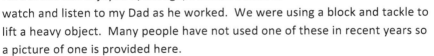 for example, when used without an awareness of the emotions of others, or used without tact and in the correct timing, can slam the door shut on someone's ideas or dreams.

Changing does not mean changing who you are, it means changing how you love.

My dad and I were working together many years ago. I was a young man, still in high school, and wasn't all that thrilled to have to spend part of my Saturday working when I could have been somewhere with my friends. Part of me still enjoyed it, though, because I liked to watch and listen to my Dad as he worked. We were using a block and tackle to lift a heavy object. Many people have not used one of these in recent years so a picture of one is provided here.

As we were lifting the object the rope broke. My immediate thought was that my work for the day was done. I underestimated my Dad's skills. He didn't seem fazed by this setback at all, and picked up the two pieces of rope and began to weave them back together. I watched in amazement at his craftsmanship as he skillfully manipulated this one-inch thick rope, weaving its two ends back together in a matter of minutes. When it was done I couldn't tell where the break had been.

"There," he said. "Good as new. In fact it's better." I knew I was about to receive another of my Dad's precious gifts: the life lessons he taught me through every day, common experiences.

"This section of rope, the part that I just weaved back together, is now the strongest part of the rope. The rope will break somewhere else before it ever breaks here again."

I marveled at my Dad. First, he possessed a skill few, if any, still have: the ability to weave a broken rope back together. More importantly, however, my Dad taught me about mending broken relationships.

Relationships between two or more people are fragile, and can be easily damaged by words or actions. This tenuous balancing act is made even more precarious by the same thing that can make our relationships so special: our unique and special personalities. All of us have distinctive likes, dislikes and peculiarities that make us extraordinary individuals. These are often, if not usually, part of what draws people together. We see something in someone else that is special, that sets them apart from others. Unfortunately, these special and unique qualities are also what often cause small and sometimes seismic rifts in our relationships.

The things that irritate one person are often not even known to the other. We're often not aware that the thing we just did or said was an incredible irritant to someone else. We can be angry for years over something someone said that hurt us, and the other person is not even aware that it hurt us at all. We are unique in our special gifts, talents and personalities. We're also unique in what hurts and causes us emotional pain.

When we hurt others, the rope of our relationship is frayed or perhaps broken. It can, however, be repaired; it can be woven back together, better than before. Our relationships can be renewed.

To renew something is to bring it fresh life. Something that is renewed is restored and transformed. Renewal is at the heart of our relationship with God. Jesus became man and died for our sins that we may be renewed. Just as our bodies are being constantly renewed as our blood is washed clean by our kidneys, our soul and spirit are washed clean by the blood of Jesus shed for us on the cross.

Therefore we do not lose heart, but though our outer man is decaying, yet our inner man is being renewed day by day. (2 Corinthians, 4:16, NAS)

We can be renewed day by day, and when we are renewed in Jesus we are in position to renew our relationships with others.

... if indeed you have heard Him and have been taught in Him, just as truth is in Jesus, that, in reference to your former manner of life, you lay aside the old self, which is being corrupted in accordance with the lusts of deceit, and that you be renewed in the spirit of your mind, and put on the new self, which in the likeness of God has been created in righteousness and holiness of the truth.
Ephesians 4:21-24, NAS

We don't have to be trapped in incorrect thinking, whether it be about ourselves, others or God. Our minds can be renewed, allowing us to be complete and whole, reflecting the image of God in which we are made.

Do not lie to one another, since you laid aside the old self with its evil practices, and have put on the new self who is being renewed to a true knowledge according to the image of the One who created him—a renewal in which there is no distinction between Greek and Jew, circumcised and uncircumcised, barbarian, Scythian, slave and freeman, but Christ is all, and in all. Colossians 3:9-11

Our new self, the one purchased for us by Jesus, is renewed. There is no distinction now between us and everyone else we are in relationship with. We are all renewed in Christ, and can renew our relationships daily.

The Webster's 1828 dictionary definition of "life" states it well. It refers to the renewal of living organisms, whether plant or animal and it says "...they are not strictly dead, till the functions of their organs are incapable of being renewed." We are not dead; we can be and are renewed through Jesus, and because we are renewed our relationships can be reconciled.

Jesus became the sacrificial lamb, the last sacrifice needed, so that we can be reconciled to Him. Forgiveness in our relationships is not ensured. It is possible that others may decide not to forgive us or to accept our forgiveness of them. They may choose to cling to their anger or their hurt. As with Adam and Eve in the very beginning, we all get to make our own decisions.

Reconciliation to God, however, is ensured. We come to Him already forgiven because of Jesus, the Gift, the final sacrificial lamb. Only a decision on our part is required.

Jesus' gift to us, His payment for our sins on the cross, made reconciliation with God the Father possible. It is the single most powerful act in history, and this model of reconciliation is the most powerful force in a relationship. It alone, not good feelings, not common interests, not lust, and not money, keeps relationships healthy and functioning. Reconciliation weaves the fibers of relationships back together; making what was once frayed or broken, now strong and reliable. The most important aspect of reconciliation is that we all need it. Anyone that is in more than just a superficial relationship with another person will, at some point and probably at many points, need to reconcile with them. This is as much a certainty as the sun rising in the morning.

The act of reconciling with another person requires specific elements. First is the desire, the intent, to reconcile. Do we really want to, or is our anger so strong that it negates the value we once saw and felt in the relationship with this other person? At one point we were drawn to them, wanting to be with them, valuing our time together. Do we even want that again? Anger is a powerful emotion, and it can produce an adrenalin-filled response that we actually enjoy. Sometimes we nurse this anger, keeping it alive, feeding it and thinking that in some way this anger is our way of getting back at the other person. In reality, this anger ultimately only affects one person: us. Instead of hurting the other person, our anger just holds us as self-incarcerated prisoners. We hold the key to the cell, but we refuse to use it.

Secondly, it will require a willingness to look inward, to examine ourselves, to see how we have contributed to the hurt and separation. It is possible that we are blameless, that we truly are victims in the situation and have done nothing to cause the emotional separation. It is possible, but it is not likely. Rifts in relationships are caused less by the cruel and thoughtless acts of one person, and more by the assumptions and lack of honest communication of two.

Finally, reconciliation requires what is perhaps the most difficult of all qualities: humility. This most-precious but overlooked and misunderstood quality is at the core of our relationships. Humility comes from the strength of knowing who you are, your good points and bad, and being strong enough to deal with them. Humility knows the weaknesses that are common to us and is not afraid to address them. It requires strength of character, resilience and determination to press onward making the changes needed in our lives, no matter how difficult. And, humility has the confidence and security to put other people and their needs ahead of our own.

Abel's gift was born out of humility. He wanted reconciliation with God, he looked at himself and saw his faults and need for change, and he humbled himself and brought a gift that would represent his true position before God. His gift of a kidney surrounded by fat showed that he knew who he was, knew his faults and weaknesses, and was willing to offer them to God in order to restore relationship. God accepted the gift, consuming it with fire, and in doing so gave a way for others to be reconciled to Him also.

The priest shall offer them up in smoke on the altar as food, an offering by fire for a soothing aroma; all fat is the LORD'S (Lev. 3:16, NAS)

The priest shall sprinkle the blood on the altar of the LORD at the doorway of the tent of meeting, and offer up the fat in smoke as a soothing aroma to the LORD (Lev. 17: 6, NAS)

Forty-four times the burning of fat is mentioned in the scripture as a pleasing or soothing aroma to God. Why? Why was this act significant? It wasn't just the smell; it was the reason behind it. The smell came from someone offering a sacrifice, a gift of reconciliation to God. It came from an act of contrition, from someone who, like Abel, recognized their human weaknesses in relation to the wonders of God. Every sacrifice to God contained the burning of fat, and every smell of burning fat meant that someone was repenting, coming back to God, coming back into relationship with Him. A son or a daughter was making the decision to draw close to their Father.

Few things are as difficult to accept, as difficult to work through, as painful, as estrangement from a child. All of us parents know the heartache and intense emotional pain felt when one of our children chooses to separate from us emotionally. They may move away, they may take a job on another continent and still remain close and connected. Or, they may live in another part of town and be completely distant and detached. God is our Father, and He knows this pain. The parable of the lost son illustrates this well.

And He said, "A man had two sons. The younger of them said to his father, 'Father, give me the share of the estate that falls to me.' So he divided his wealth between them. And not many days later, the younger son gathered everything together and went on a journey into a distant country, and there he squandered his estate with loose living. Now when he had spent everything, a severe famine occurred in that country, and he began to be impoverished. So he went and hired himself out to one of the citizens of that country, and he sent him into his fields to feed swine. And he would have gladly filled his stomach with the pods that the swine were eating, and no one was giving anything to him. But when he came to his senses, he said, 'How many of my father's hired men have more than enough bread, but I am dying here with hunger! I will get up and go to my father, and will say to him, "Father, I have sinned against heaven, and in your sight; I am no longer worthy to be called your son; make me as one of your hired men."' So he got up and came to his father. But while he was still a long way off, his father saw him and felt compassion for him, and ran and embraced him and kissed him. And the son said to him, 'Father, I have sinned against heaven and in your sight; I am no longer worthy to be called your son.' But the father said to his slaves, 'Quickly bring out the best robe and put it on him, and put a ring on his hand and sandals on his feet; and bring the fattened calf, kill it, and let us eat and celebrate; for this son of mine was dead and has come to life again; he was lost and has been found.' And they began to celebrate. (Luke 15:11-24, NAS)

This story is about a young man and his decision to take his inheritance early, leave home and live on his own. He ends up wasting his money, becoming poor and destitute. It speaks of this young man's change of heart and his decision to return home. It speaks of the father's joy in seeing the return of his son. It also speaks of a father's pain.

Verse 20 says, *So he* (the son) *got up and came to his father. But while he was still a long way off, his father saw him and felt compassion for him, and ran and embraced him and kissed him.*

The father saw his son coming and *felt compassion* for him. The English translation of this word does not begin to do it justice. The Greek word used here is *splagchnizomai*[59] and one of the meanings is to have your bowels ache.

---

[59] Strong's Hebrew Greek Dictionary: G4697

94

While this may not be a very pretty definition, it is a very apt one. All of us parents who have every worried about our children have felt this pain. It is a pain so intense it seems to be coming from the very core of our being. We long for our son or our daughter to be okay, to be safe, to return home. Our stomachs churn, our heads ache, our bowels ache. Our entire beings are hurting with the concern for our children.

This is only a small fraction of the concern, the pain, the love that our Heavenly Father feels for us. This is why God accepted Abel's gift. He saw a son returning to Him. He accepted this gift, and accepts our gift of repentance, of turning back to Him. This is a certainty. It will never fail.

God desires that we have a close, loving relationship with Him, and with each other. We can, but it will take work and honest decisions by everyone involved. If we choose to humble ourselves, to work toward honest growth and change, to care for others as we care for ourselves, the problems we now face in our relationships can become testimonies of love and forgiveness to our children, friends, family member, coworkers, and anyone else that hears our story.

Reconciliation. No smell could have been sweeter.

12. Freedom with Wholeness

The house was somewhat cool as he walked into the kitchen for his morning cup of coffee. It was a bright, crisp fall morning, the kind that seems to pull out the emotions of happiness, security and contentment. There could be no more perfect place than this: his own home, having coffee in the kitchen with the warm sunshine lighting up the room – and her. He didn't speak at first; he just looked at her, standing at the stove, making something for breakfast, apparently for him. He never got tired of looking at her; often "stealing" glances at her as she went about her daily routines. She was truly a beautiful woman, even after 29, no; it was now 30 years of marriage.

He never imagined marriage could be like this. He and his wife truly loved each other. They loved spending time together, doing things and going places together. If one was doing something the other wanted to do it too. They truly were best friends. There were the occasional miscommunications and misunderstandings. Tempers sometimes flared and they certainly had many moments, even after all these years, where they clearly didn't understand each other; but none of that mattered. Working through whatever issues came up was part of the joy of being married to her.

How could he be so lucky?

Mark

They sat at the table eating dinner, the three of them, like they had so many times before. Mark was home for the weekend; his freshman year of college off to a good start. The conversation drifted from one topic to another. Mark talked about things happening on campus; his dad spoke about work, some things were going well, some were challenging; two guys had been laid off and there could be more. His mom mentioned a project she was involved in at church.

"I neglected to take care of something," his dad said, "and I need to do it now."

Mark looked at his mom, not sure where this was going.

"Mark, you are a remarkable young man, not because you are doing well in school, although I'm really proud of you for that..."

Mark's mom smiled at him as if she already knew what was coming next.

"...you are remarkable because of how strong you are, how courageous, and how much you love your mother and me. The night you spoke to us and told us how much we were hurting you when we hurt each other changed our lives. We had no idea. You gave us the opportunity to change. Our relationship is better than it ever has been. Thank you."

Mark just smiled. It was good to be home.

Samantha

"Can I have the car for a little while tonight?" Samantha asked her mom.

Her mom looked at her, perhaps a little warily. "Where do you want to go?"

"I want to spend more time with Janet. She's still not doing well and I'm worried about her and I want to hang out with her. She's fun to be with when she isn't drinking or doing other things."

Samantha's mom hesitated. She didn't want a daughter that just obeyed rules. She knew that sometimes situations fell outside of the rules and mature decisions needed to be made. These were the decisions of life, and she wanted Samantha to be prepared for them. She needed to give Samantha opportunities to make good decisions and to be trusted.

"Sure," she answered. "Where do you think you'll go?"

"Actually, I thought I'd bring her over here."

Amy

The staff meeting was a difficult one. There were a lot of challenging issues facing the company and they needed to be addressed. The attitudes and spirits in the room were high, however, as people brainstormed on possible solutions. The atmosphere was conducive to their creativity.

"Let's hear some of the ideas you've come up with in your groups," Ted said. "Amy, why don't you start us off. What has your group come up with?"

"We discussed ways we can strengthen our position in the 40 to 50 year old demographic group," Amy began. "Our focus has been on the younger groups and we think this is a market that has a lot of potential for us."

Ted appeared to be listening thoughtfully and didn't reply for a moment or two.

"I'm not sure on that direction," he began. "We've targeted that group before and not had great success."

Amy waited, wondering if this is where he would insert a comment or joke that would leave her feeling ridiculed in front of the others again.

"Go ahead with this, though," Ted continued. "You might be right and maybe you'll come up with something we haven't thought of before." He smiled at her as he said it.

Freedom. It is a multifaceted concept. Individuals, groups and entire countries long for it, fight for it, and die for it, but what does it mean for us in our everyday world, what is freedom for us in our daily lives? It does not exist because of a piece of paper or a presidential decree. Real freedom, the freedom that touches us where we live, exists when we are whole and are able to fully be who we are designed to be, and God has designed us to be with, work with and love others. We are not free because we are alone and independent; we are free when we have strong relationships with others, and when we commit to working through the problems that inevitably arise.

We will never be whole without relationships because it is only through close relationships with other people that we discover our strengths, weaknesses and human frailties.

We find freedom in our relationships when we work through the problems. It is the problems themselves, the very things that we often try so hard to avoid, that help us learn more about ourselves and others. True freedom isn't a lack of restrictions or laws; it is being able to function fully, completely vibrant and whole, reflecting God in His love and compassion for others.

God made man to be free, to feel His love, and to express it to others, and real love is only expressed and felt when it is given through our free choice. Real love cannot be forced, required, or be a result of following commands. Healthy, loving relationships are formed when two people are able to function freely, learning how to value and appreciate themselves first and then each other as God's special creation.

Abel was named by his parents as emptiness, vanity, and unsatisfactory. He was human, vain and empty, probably self-centered and arrogant. Abel was probably a lot like us.

Abel is also the man that is later described as faithful and righteous.[60] He is now known not with the identity his parents gave him, but with the character that developed in him. He changed. He grew. He saw his weaknesses, his shortcomings, and recognized his need for God's cleansing and forgiveness and he brought a gift for all to see that represented just that. His gift of repentance was accepted and God forgave him, and they were reconciled in a way that cannot be changed. God lifted Abel's guilt, changing his image forever.

This same opportunity exists for all of us. We are free to fail and we are free to succeed. We are free to be reconciled to God, and to others, by doing exactly what Abel did: examine ourselves, see our faults, ask for forgiveness, and feel the burden of our guilt being lifted off.

---

[60] Matthew 32:35, Hebrew 11:4

Real change can't be forced upon us or be a result solely of our hard work or because someone else thinks we need it. Real change comes from knowing and becoming who we really are. We are God's creation, made from His love and in His image. It is a two-part experience: we know that God loves us, and this knowledge frees us to accept others and ourselves as wonderful creations of a loving Father. A feeling flows from this revelation that can be both infective and attractive. It is infective because others see and feel the confidence that comes from knowing we are loved and accepted, just the way we are, warts and all. It infuses others with the desire to know this kind of love and close relationship. It is attractive because others sense the beauty that comes from being unconditionally loved by God. Love has been received and so love can now pour out freely. A person's life has been changed, not through rigid accounts of restriction and discipline, but through the freedom felt in God's unconditional love.

Relationship with God. It sounds nice, but it also sounds somewhat ethereal. What kind of relationship can we have with the One who is the Creator of the Universe? What kind of relationship would that be? What kind of relationship does God really want with us? The answer is found in the deepest relationship forged between a man and a woman: God wants an intimate relationship with us.

When a man and a woman are intimate they become one flesh.[61] Popular culture and media have reduced it to just a physical act, a mere gesture between friends or even acquaintances. Nothing could be further from the truth. True intimacy requires joining the other person emotionally, mentally and spiritually as well as physically. Joining another person intimately is to give yourself to them completely, holding nothing back. The two people are forever joined in body and in spirit. It requires true openness and understanding. There can be nothing left unknown or unseen, both physically and emotionally.

Intimacy between people is a three-step process involving honesty, openness and acceptance. Remove any of these three and intimacy is reduced to rote actions. Abel's gift of kidneys surrounded by fat perfectly illustrates these

---

[61] Gen. 2:24

three ingredients as he sought to be restored to an intimate relationship with God.

He was honest with himself, seeing all of his faults, weaknesses, thoughts and desires, and came before God just as he was, Abel, the vain one. Before we can enter into any intimate relationship with God or anyone else, we have to be willing to honestly examine ourselves to see what is there; the good and the bad.

Abel's gift also demonstrates the next key ingredient of openness. Abel was open with God, showing through this gift that he was a man with issues and needed help. The kidneys represented the constant cleansing that Abel knew he required and could only get from God. The gift was a demonstration of Abel's human condition and proper position before his Creator. Abel had to have examined his life honestly, taking a real and accurate appraisal and decided that changes needed to be made. He saw his need for God's restoring powers, and then was open before his God, coming to Him in full disclosure, withholding nothing.

Intimacy does not occur without the third ingredient: acceptance. Abel honestly examined his life and his character and saw the need for change. He openly came before God with those faults and frailties in full view. God then accepted Abel the way he was. Abel's gift was a representation of his need for relationship with God. It clearly showed Abel's need for constant cleansing. It was honest; it was open, and it was accepted. God didn't require Abel to reach a specific level of maturity or growth. He didn't tell Abel to come back later when he had grown up more. He didn't expect Abel to be like Him; God accepted Abel as he was, a fallen and flawed man that just wanted relationship.

The process of intimacy looks like this:

Honesty

We first look inward to honestly appraise our character, emotions and desires. Willingly we examine our strengths as well as our faults

---

↓

Openness.

These strengths and weaknesses of character, these desires and emotions are shared openly with the other person.

↓

Acceptance.

We are accepted by the other person just as we are.

↓

Intimacy

This does not mean that we are to divulge every aspect of our lives with all of our friends and acquaintances. We don't share the deepest parts of our thoughts and emotions with everyone we know. These areas of our lives are personal and private, and only meant to be shared with those with whom we are truly intimate.

The process of intimacy is the same now for us as it for Abel. We can go to church, sing the songs, raise our hands and say the prayers, but without these three key ingredients there is no intimacy with God.

We cannot be truly intimate with someone without feeling understood and valued. Intimate relationship brings feelings of validity, affirmation and acceptance. Guilt and shame are eradicated, replaced by love and acceptance.

This is the type of relationship God wants with us. He wants us to join with Him completely, holding nothing back. He desires to know us and for us to know Him completely, for us to know that we are understood by Him. He knows all of our faults, all of the thoughts we think we can keep hidden from Him, all of our selfish and hurtful actions, and He loves us. We stand naked before Him, with all of our problems and faults exposed, and He accepts us.

This is where all loving relationships begin: with us being deeply loved by God. Intimacy with God, giving all to Him, holding nothing back, brings the satisfaction, the peace, the contentment and the understanding that are necessary for us to love others.

Can we have full, loving and meaningful relationships with other human beings that, like us, can be difficult to like, let alone love? Yes. These can become the rule rather than the exception. Becoming a whole person requires loving others, and loving others begins with us loving God and allowing Him to love us. God's love for us is greater than we can possibly imagine. It is bigger than rituals or formulas, bigger than lists of things we can and cannot do, bigger than our faults that expose themselves daily, bigger than the expectations of ourselves or others, and bigger than the feelings of shame and disgrace that we feel when we fail God yet again. Abel knew this. His very name told him he was unworthy. He knew this to be true, he was unworthy, but he also knew his God's love for him was greater than his unworthiness.

Healthy, loving relationships. They shouldn't be that difficult, but they are. At times it seems as though the concept is too ideal, just a nice idea that can't really exist in our everyday world. This is not the way God intended it.

God created us and put us on this earth because He loves us. No other reason. He doesn't need us. We don't have to earn His love and acceptance. He is love and He loves us. He also wants us to show that love to others, and this is where things break down. We, mankind, have had difficulty with relationships from the very beginning. We have messed up since life in the Garden and we continue to mess up on a daily basis. We don't grow up in environments that display God's love to others in perfect ways. At best we get a version that is somewhat diluted with our human proclivity towards self-seeking behavior, and at worst is negligent and abusive. How then do we learn to love, get along with, work with and live with others that are just as messed up as we are? We learn from the only true source of love. We learn from God. We can only have healthy, loving relationships with others by knowing God's love first.

God's interactions with His first family demonstrated how His perfect love could be applied to imperfect creatures like us. He modeled His love in action. We can use that same model as we attempt to live our lives in close relationships with those around us.

He showed us that things happen to us that are outside of our control, that aren't our fault, but even in these circumstances we can make the decision to love others.

Consequences for hurtful behavior and disobedience can be meted out with care and compassion, equipping people to live better in the future, as God did with Adam and Eve.

We are free creatures: free to make our own decisions, free to love others, but also free to be mean and hurtful. We are also free to forgive those who make these poor decisions.

God showed us how objective guilt, the guilt that is from Him and tells us when we have truly done something wrong, can be a tool to help us turn to each other and ask for forgiveness.

Repentance and forgiveness bring freedom to both parties involved. They are the keys to getting out of our self-imposed emotional prisons. We can forgive others without requiring any action from them. Our forgiveness is not dependent on someone else saying, "I'm sorry." It is ours to freely give.

It is only in close relationships that forgiveness works. Forgiveness from a stranger has very little meaning for us; it is the forgiveness from those close to us, from family, spouses and close friends that impacts our lives. Forgiveness, like the fat surrounding the kidneys, offers the protection, care and support needed for the difficulties we face together.

God's design of our bodies is a clear example of our constant need of cleansing. He is there to remove the many unhealthy and damaging emotional "toxins" we take in through the course of daily living. We provide this same "cleansing" for each other as the closeness of our relationships brings honesty and open communication.

Growth and change are necessary components for life, including our emotional, mental and spiritual lives. Without them we remain stagnant, mired in the same bog of immature and hurtful thinking.

Reconciliation, to God and to each other, is the method through which we mend broken relationships, weaving them back together and producing even stronger bonds than we had before. It is a sweet smell to God.

The biggest lesson we learn from God's first family, however, is that we are loved. God loved Adam and Eve even when they were disobedient and rebellious. The consequences of their sin were enacted, but with love and compassion. The same is true for us, all of us, today.

If you lose your temper, God still loves you.

If you cheat on your income tax, God still loves you.

If you hurt someone with your words or actions, God still loves you.

If you are impatient and criticize others, God still loves you.

If you are disobedient and rebellious, God still loves you.

There is nothing you have to do, or can do, to earn His love. You don't have to say extra prayers, sing certain songs, or even go to church meetings. All these things can be good, but they are things you can choose to do because you want to, not because you have to. Knowing God's love is not about what you have to do, it's about what you are free to do because you are loved.

The eagle that flies, the horse that runs, the baby that cries, are all giving honor to God just by doing what they are created to do. Nothing else is required.

We have the freedom to be vibrant and healthy in our interactions with others, expressing fully the image of God. Freedom comes when we can be more of who we are designed to be without withdrawing, becoming "pale" or afraid. Life was given to us by God to be an expression of learning and failing, loving and grieving, and more than all, caring about other people that are struggling to do the same. Life wasn't designed to be easy. Thorns and thistles will grow. They were not a new creation for mankind to deal with because someone had a failure. Thorns and thistles had been created along with roses and tulips. God created them all. We are capable of managing over uncomfortable situations with skill and sensitivity as we learn how to care for others the way God cares for us.

The key to becoming whole, to living a whole and complete life, is to first know that you are loved. We are difficult people, all of us, and we are loved.

How can we love difficult people? By knowing God, the source of love, first.

Herein is love, not that we loved God, but that He loved us and sent His son to be the propitiation for our sins. Beloved, if God so loved us, we ought also to love one another. No man has seen God at any time. If we love one another God dwelleth in us, and His love is perfected in us. (1John: 4: 10-12, NAS)

Appendix

1. Cummings, et all, 1985
    The influence of others' emotions on the emotions and aggression of 2-year-old children was examined. Dyads of familiar peers were exposed during play to a sequence of experimental manipulations of background emotions of warmth and anger. Children readily distinguished between the prosocial and angry interactions of unfamiliar adults. Typically they responded to the angry verbal exchange with some form of distress. Exposure to angry adult interactions was associated also with subsequent increases in aggression between peers. A second exposure to the enactment of anger a month later resulted in still higher levels of distress and aggression. Children's response patterns were suggestive of process mediated by emotional reactivity rather than a behavioral modeling influence. Boys showed more aggression than girls following the simulation of anger, where as girls showed more distress than boys during the simulation. There was some evidence for stability and continuity in individual patterns of response. The theoretical and practical implications of such pronounced sensitivity to others' conflicts and interpersonal problems in young children are considered.

2. Dr. John Ratey, *Spark: The Revolutionary New Science of Exercise and the Brain*. The way you choose to cope with stress can change not only how you feel, but also how it transforms the brain. If you react passively or if there is simply no way out, stress can become damaging. Like most psychiatric issues, chronic stress results from the brain getting locked into the same pattern, typically one marked by pessimism, fear and retreat. (p. 60)

    From what we've since learned about the biology of stress and recovery, stress seems to have an effect on the brain similar to that of vaccines on the immune system. In limited doses it causes brain cells to overcompensate and thus gird themselves against future demands. Neuroscientists call this phenomenon stress inoculation. (p. 61)

    If mild stress becomes chronic, the unrelenting cascade of cortisol triggers genetic actions that begin to sever synaptic connections and cause dendrites to atrophy and cells to die; eventually the hippocampus can end up physically shriveled, like a raison. (p. 74)

And anybody, regardless of their nature and upbringing, will exhibit the ill effects of chronic stress if there is no outlet for frustration, no sense of control, no social support. (p. 75)

Monica Starkman at the University of Michigan studies Cushing's syndrome, an endocrine dysfunction in which the body is continually flooded with cortisol. The scientific name for the disorder sp3eaks volumes: hypercortisolism. Its sym0ptioms are eerily similar to those of chronic stress: weight gain around the midsection; breaking down muscle tissue to produce unnecessary glucose and then fat; insulin resistance and possibly diabetes; panic attacks, anxiety, depression, and increased reis of heart disease. (p. 76)

3.   Gen 2:7-25 MSG
     GOD formed Man out of dirt from the ground and blew into his nostrils the breath of life. The Man came alive--a living soul!
     Then GOD planted a garden in Eden, in the east. He put the Man he had just made in it.
     GOD made all kinds of trees grow from the ground, trees beautiful to look at and good to eat. The Tree-of-Life was in the middle of the garden, also the Tree-of-Knowledge-of-Good-and-Evil.
     A river flows out of Eden to water the garden and from there divides into four rivers.
     The first is named Pishon; it flows through Havilah where there is gold.
     The gold of this land is good. The land is also known for a sweet-scented resin and the onyx stone.
     The second river is named Gihon; it flows through the land of Cush.
     The third river is named Hiddekel and flows east of Assyria. The fourth river is the Euphrates.
     GOD took the Man and set him down in the Garden of Eden to work the ground and keep it in order.
     GOD commanded the Man, "You can eat from any tree in the garden, except from the Tree-of-Knowledge-of-Good-and-Evil. Don't eat from it. The moment you eat from that tree, you're dead."
     GOD said, "It's not good for the Man to be alone; I'll make him a helper, a companion."
     So GOD formed from the dirt of the ground all the animals of the field and all the birds of the air. He brought them to the Man to see what he would name them. Whatever the Man called each living creature, that was its name.
     The Man named the cattle, named the birds of the air, named the wild animals; but he didn't find a suitable companion.
     GOD put the Man into a deep sleep. As he slept he removed one of his ribs and replaced it with flesh.
     GOD then used the rib that he had taken from the Man to make Woman and presented her to the Man.

The Man said, "Finally! Bone of my bone, flesh of my flesh! Name her Woman for she was made from Man."

Therefore a man leaves his father and mother and embraces his wife. They become one flesh.

The two of them, the Man and his Wife, were naked, but they felt no shame.

4. Gen 3:1-24 MSG

The serpent was clever, more clever than any wild animal GOD had made. He spoke to the Woman: "Do I understand that God told you not to eat from any tree in the garden?"

The Woman said to the serpent, "Not at all. We can eat from the trees in the garden.

It's only about the tree in the middle of the garden that God said, 'Don't eat from it; don't even touch it or you'll die.'"

The serpent told the Woman, "You won't die.

God knows that the moment you eat from that tree, you'll see what's really going on. You'll be just like God, knowing everything, ranging all the way from good to evil."

When the Woman saw that the tree looked like good eating and realized what she would get out of it--she'd know everything!--she took and ate the fruit and then gave some to her husband, and he ate. Immediately the two of them did "see what's really going on"--saw themselves naked! They sewed fig leaves together as makeshift clothes for themselves. When they heard the sound of GOD strolling in the garden in the evening breeze, the Man and his Wife hid in the trees of the garden, hid from GOD.

GOD called to the Man: "Where are you?"

He said, "I heard you in the garden and I was afraid because I was naked. And I hid."

GOD said, "Who told you you were naked? Did you eat from that tree I told you not to eat from?"

The Man said, "The Woman you gave me as a companion, she gave me fruit from the tree, and, yes, I ate it."

GOD said to the Woman, "What is this that you've done?" "The serpent seduced me," she said, "and I ate."

GOD told the serpent: "Because you've done this, you're cursed, cursed beyond all cattle and wild animals, cursed to slink on your belly and eat dirt all your life.

I'm declaring war between you and the Woman, between your offspring and hers. He'll wound your head, you'll wound his heel."

He told the Woman: "I'll multiply your pains in childbirth; you'll give birth to your babies in pain. You'll want to please your husband, but he'll lord it over you."

He told the Man: "Because you listened to your wife and ate from the tree That I commanded you not to eat from, 'Don't eat from this tree,' The very ground is cursed because of you; getting food from the ground Will be as painful as having babies is for your wife; you'll be working in pain all your life long.

The ground will sprout thorns and weeds, you'll get your food the hard way, Planting and tilling and harvesting, sweating in the fields from dawn to dusk, Until you return to that ground yourself, dead and buried; you started out as dirt, you'll end up dirt."

The Man, known as Adam, named his wife Eve because she was the mother of all the living.

GOD made leather clothing for Adam and his wife and dressed them.

GOD said, "The Man has become like one of us, capable of knowing everything, ranging from good to evil. What if he now should reach out and take fruit from the Tree-of-Life and eat, and live forever? Never--this cannot happen!"

So GOD expelled them from the Garden of Eden and sent them to work the ground, the same dirt out of which they'd been made.

He threw them out of the garden and stationed angel-cherubim and a revolving sword of fire east of it, guarding the path to the Tree-of-Life.

5. Jer. 17:10

    But I, GOD, search the heart and examine the mind. I get to the heart of the human. I get to the root of things. I treat them as they really are, not as they pretend to be."

6. Ps. 7:9, KJV

    Oh let the wickedness of the wicked come to an end; but establish the just: for the righteous God trieth the hearts and reins.

    Ps 73:21, KJV
    Thus my heart was grieved, and I was pricked in my reins.

Chapter 2   Who Can I Blame?

7. Gen 4:1-2

    Now the man had relations with his wife Eve, and she conceived and gave birth to Cain, and she said, "I have gotten a manchild with the help of the LORD." Again, she gave birth to his brother Abel. And Abel was a keeper of flocks, but Cain was a tiller of the ground. (NAS)

8. Gen 3:18

    "Both thorns and thistles it shall grow for you; And you will eat the plants of the field; (NAS)

9. Gen 3:19
    By the sweat of your face You will eat bread, Till you return to the ground,
    Because from it you were taken; For you are dust, And to dust you shall
    return." (NAS)

10. Strong Hebrew and Greek Dictionary
    Abel
    H1893
    הבל
    hebel
    heh'-bel
    The same as H1892; Hebel, the son of Adam: - Abel.
    H1892
    הבל   הבל
    hebel   hăbêl
    heh'-bel, hab-ale'

    From H1891; emptiness or vanity; figuratively something transitory and
    unsatisfactory; often used as an adverb: - X altogether, vain, vanity.
    H1891
    הבל
    hâbal
    aw-bal'

    A primitive root; to be vain in act, word, or expectation; specifically to lead
    astray: - be (become, make) vain.

11. Strong's Hebrew and Greek Dictionary
    Cain
    H7014
    קין
    qayin
    kah'-yin

    The same as H7013 (with a play upon the affinity to H7069); Kajin, the name of
    the first child, also of a place in Palestine, and of an Oriental tribe: - Cain,
    Kenite (-s).
    H7013
    קין
    qayin
    kah'-yin

    From H6969 in the original sense of fixity; a lance (as striking fast): - spear.

12. Albert Barnes notes on the Bible
    Knowledge and understanding
    <u>Gen 2:16-17</u>
    And the Lord God commanded the man, saying. - This is a pregnant sentence.
    It involves the first principles of our intellectual and moral philosophy.

    I. The command here given in words brings into activity the intellectual nature
    of man. First, the power of understanding language is called forth. The
    command here addressed to him by his Maker is totally different from the
    blessings addressed to the animals in the preceding chapter. It was not
    necessary that these blessings should be understood in order to be carried into
    effect, inasmuch as He who pronounced them gave the instincts and powers
    requisite to their accomplishment. But this command addressed to man in
    words must be understood in order to be obeyed. The capacity for
    understanding language, then, was originally lodged in the constitution of
    man, and only required to be called out by the articulate voice of God. Still
    there is something wonderful here, something beyond the present grasp and
    promptitude of human apprehension. If we accept the blessing, which may not
    have been heard, or may not have been uttered before this command, these
    words were absolutely the first that were heard by man.

    The significance of the sentences they formed must have been at the same
    time conveyed to man by immediate divine teaching. How the lesson was
    taught in an instant of time we cannot explain, though we have a distant
    resemblance of it in an infant learning to understand its mother-tongue. This
    process, indeed, goes over a space of two years; but still there is an instant in
    which the first conception of a sign is formed, the first word is apprehended,
    the first sentence is understood. In that instant the knowledge of language is
    virtually attained. With man, created at once in his full though undeveloped
    powers, and still unaffected by any moral taint, this instant came with the first
    words spoken to his ear and to his soul by his Maker's impressive voice, and
    the first lesson of language was at once thoroughly taught and learned. Man is
    now master of the theory of speech; the conception of a sign has been
    conveyed into his mind. This is the passive lesson of elocution: the practice,
    the active lesson, will speedily follow.

    Not only the secondary part, however, but at the same time the primary and
    fundamental part of man's intellectual nature is here developed. The
    understanding of the sign necessarily implies the knowledge of the thing
    signified. The objective is represented here by the "trees of the garden." The

subjective comes before his mind in the pronoun "thou." The physical constitution of man appears in the process of "eating." The moral part of his nature comes out in the significance of the words "mayest" and "shalt not." The distinction of merit in actions and things is expressed in the epithets "good and evil." The notion of reward is conveyed in the terms "life" and "death." And, lastly, the presence and authority of "the Lord God" is implied in the very nature of a command. Here is at least the opening of a wide field of observation for the nascent powers of the mind. He, indeed, must bear the image of God in perceptive powers, who shall scan with heedful eye the loftiest as well as the lowest in these varied scenes of reality. But as with the sign, so with the thing signified, a glance of intelligence instantaneously begins the converse of the susceptible mind with the world of reality around, and the enlargement of the sphere of human knowledge is merely a matter of time without end. How rapidly the process of apprehension would go on in the opening dawn of man's intellectual activity, how many flashes of intelligence would be compressed into a few moments of his first consciousness, we cannot tell. But we can readily believe that he would soon be able to form a just yet an infantile conception of the varied themes which are presented to his mind in this brief command.

Thus, the susceptible part of man's intellect is evoked. The conceptive part will speedily follow, and display itself in the many inventions that will be sought out and applied to the objects, which are placed at his disposal.

13. Adam Clark's Commentary on the Bible
    Genesis 3:6
    The tree was good for food -

    • The fruit appeared to be wholesome and nutritive. And that it was pleasant to the eyes.

    • The beauty of the fruit tended to whet and increase appetite. And a tree to be desired to make one wise, which was,

    • An additional motive to please the palate.

From these three sources all natural and moral evil sprang: they are exactly what the apostle calls the desire of the flesh; the tree was good for food: the desire of the eye; it was pleasant to the sight: and the pride of life; it was a tree to be desired to make one wise. God had undoubtedly created our first parents not only very wise and intelligent, but also with a great capacity and suitable propensity to increase in knowledge. Those who think that Adam was created so perfect as to preclude the possibility of his increase in knowledge have taken a very false view of the subject. We shall certainly be convinced that our first parents were in a state of sufficient perfection when we consider,

- That they were endued with a vast capacity to obtain knowledge.

- That all the means of information were within their reach.

- That there was no hindrance to the most direct conception of occurring truth.

- That all the objects of knowledge, whether natural or moral, were ever at hand.

- That they had the strongest propensity to know; and,

- The greatest pleasure in knowing.

To have God and nature continually open to the view of the soul; and to have a soul capable of viewing both, and fathoming endlessly their unbounded glories and excellences, without hindrance or difficulty; what a state of perfection! What a consummation of bliss! This was undoubtedly the state and condition of our first parents; even the present ruins of the state are incontestable evidences of its primitive excellence. We see at once how transgression came; it was natural for them to desire to be increasingly wise. God had implanted this desire in their minds; but he showed them that this desire should be gratified in a certain way; that prudence and judgment should always regulate it; that they should carefully examine what God had opened to their view; and should not pry into what he chose to conceal. He alone who knows all things knows how much knowledge the soul needs to its perfection and increasing happiness, in what subjects this may be legitimately sought, and where the mind may make excursions and discoveries to its prejudice and ruin. There are doubtless many subjects, which angels are capable of knowing, and which God chooses to conceal even from them, because that knowledge would tend neither to their perfection nor happiness. Of every attainment and object of pursuit it may be said, in the words of an ancient poet, who conceived correctly on the subject, and expressed his thoughts with perspicuity and energy: -

"There is a rule for all things; there are in fine fixed and stated limits, on either side of which righteousness cannot be found." On the line of duty alone we must walk.

Such limits God certainly assigned from the beginning: Thou shalt come up to this; thou shalt not pass it. And as he assigned the limits, so he assigned the means. It is lawful for thee to acquire knowledge in this way; it is unlawful to seek it in that. And had he not a right to do so? And would his creation have been perfect without it?

Chapter 3   Finding Truth

14. Strong's Hebrew and Greek Dictionary
     Truth
     H571
     אמת
     'emeth
     eh'-meth

     Contracted from H539; stability; figuratively certainty, truth, trustworthiness: - assured (-ly), establishment, faithful, right, sure, true (-ly, -th), verity.

15. Strong's Hebrew and Greek Dictionary
     Yea
     H637
     אף
     'aph
     af

     A primitive particle; meaning accession (used as an adverb or conjugation); also or yea; adversatively though: - also, + although, and (furthermore, yet), but, even, + how much less (more, rather than), moreover, with, yea.

16. Strong's Hebrew and Greek Dictionary
     Indeed
     H3588
     כי
     kîy
     kee

     A primitive particle (the full form of the prepositional prefix) indicating causal relations of all kinds, antecedent or consequent; (by implication) very widely used as a relative conjugation or adverb; often largely modified by other particles annexed: - and, + (forasmuch, inasmuch, where-) as, assured [-ly], + but, certainly, doubtless, + else, even, + except, for, how, (because, in, so, than) that, + nevertheless, now, rightly, seeing, since, surely, then, therefore, + (al-) though, + till, truly, + until, when, whether, while, who, yea, yet,

17. Strong's Hebrew and Greek Dictionary
God
Elohym
H430
אלהים
'ĕlôhîym
el-o-heem'

Plural of H433; gods in the ordinary sense; but specifically used (in the plural thus, magistrates; and sometimes as a superlative: - angels, X exceeding, God (gods) (-dess, -

18. Jean Piaget, translated by Margaret Cook, 1954

If the assimilation of reality to the subject's schemata involves their continuous accommodation, assimilation is no less opposed to any new accommodation, that is, to any differentiation of schemata by environmental conditions not encountered up to then. On the other hand, if accommodation prevails, that is, if the schema is differentiated, it marks the start of new assimilations. Every acquisition of accommodation becomes material for assimilation, but assimilation always resists new accommodations. It is this situation which explains the diversity of form of equilibrium between the two processes, according to whether one envisages the point of departure or the destiny of their development. P. 353

19. CS Lewis (n.d.). BrainyQuote.com. Retrieved May 18, 2013, from BrainyQuote.com Web site: http://www.brainyquote.com/quotes/quotes/c/cslewis141015.html

Chapter 4   Freedom to Fail

20. Woolfolk, Anita. Educational Psychology (2012). Pearson Education, Inc. Upper Saddle River, New Jersey. 12th Edition. Page 46

    Preoperational children, according to Piaget, have a tendency to be egocentric, to see the world and the experiences of others from their own viewpoint. The concept of egocentrism, as Piaget intended it, does not mean selfish; it simply means children often assume that everyone else shares their feelings, reactions, and perspectives. For example, if a little girl at this stage is afraid of dogs, she may assume that all children share this fear.

21. Woolfolk, Anita. Educational Psychology (2012) Pearson Education, Inc. Upper Saddle River, New Jersey. 12th Edition. Page 99

    By the time they are 2 or 3 years old, children are beginning to develop a theory of mind, an understanding that other people are people too, with their own minds, thoughts, feelings, beliefs, desires, and perceptions.

22. Random House Dictionary
    Instinct
    An inborn pattern of activity or tendency to action common to a given biological species.

23. Albert Barnes' Notes on the Bible
    Gen 2:16-17 continued:

    II. First. Next, the moral part of man's nature is here called into play. Mark God's mode of teaching. He issues a command. This is required in order to bring forth into consciousness the hitherto latent sensibility to moral obligation which was laid in the original constitution of man's being. A command implies a superior, whose right it is to command, and an inferior, whose duty it is to obey. The only ultimate and absolute ground of supremacy is creating, and of inferiority, being created. The Creator is the only proper and entire owner; and, within legitimate bounds, the owner has the right to do what he will with his own. The laying on of this command, therefore, brings man to the recognition of his dependence for being and for the character of that being on his Maker. From the knowledge of the fundamental relation of the creature to the Creator springs an immediate sense of the obligation he is under to render implicit obedience to the Author of his being. This is, therefore, man's first lesson in morals. It calls up in his breast the sense of duty, of right, of responsibility. These feelings could not have been elicited unless the moral susceptibility had been laid in the soul, and only waited for the first command to awaken it into consciousness. This lesson, however, is only the incidental effect of the command, and not the primary ground of its imposition.

Second. The special mandate here given is not arbitrary in its form, as is sometimes hastily supposed, but absolutely essential to the legal adjustment of things in this new stage of creation. Antecedent to the behest of the Creator, the only indefeasible right to all the creatures lay in himself. These creatures may be related to one another. In the great system of things, through the wonderful wisdom of the grand Designer, the use of some may be needful to the well-being, the development, and perpetuation of others. Nevertheless, no one has a shadow of right in the original nature of things to the use of any other. And when a moral agent comes upon the stage of being, in order to mark out the sphere of his legitimate action, an explicit declaration of the rights over other creatures granted and reserved must be made. The very issue of the command proclaims man's original right of property to be, not inherent, but derived.

As might be expected in these circumstances, the command has two clauses, - a permissive and a prohibitive. "Of every tree of the garden thou mayst freely eat." This displays in conspicuous terms the benignity of the Creator. "But of the tree of the knowledge of good and evil thou shalt not eat." This signalizes the absolute right of the Creator over all the trees, and over man himself. One tree only is withheld, which, whatever were its qualities, was at all events not necessary to the well-being of man. All the others that were likely for sight and good for food, including the tree of life, are made over to him by free grant. In this original provision for the vested rights of man in creation, we cannot but acknowledge with gratitude and humility the generous and considerate bounty of the Creator. This is not more conspicuous in the bestowment of all the other trees than in the withholding of the one, the participation of which was fraught with evil to mankind.

Third. The prohibitory part of this enactment is not a matter of indifference, as is sometimes imagined, but indispensable to the nature of a command, and, in particular, of a permissive act or declaration of granted rights. Every command has a negative part, expressed or implied, without which it would be no command at all. The command, "Go work today in my vineyard," implies thou shalt not do anything else; otherwise the son who works not obeys as well as the son who works. The present address of God to Adam, without the exceptive clause, would be a mere license, and not a command. But with the exceptive clause it is a command, and tantamount in meaning to the following positive injunction: Thou mayest eat of these trees only. An edict of license with a restrictive clause is the mildest form of command that could have been imposed for the trial of human obedience. Some may have thought that it would have been better for man if there had been no tree of the knowledge of good and evil.

But second thoughts will correct this rash and wrong conclusion. First. This tree may have had other purposes to serve in the economy of things of which we are not aware; and, if so, it could not have been absent without detriment to the general good. Second. But without any supposition at all, the tree was fraught with no evil whatever to man in itself. It was in the first instance the instrument of great good, of the most precious kind, to him. It served the purpose of calling up into view out of the depths of his nature the notion of moral obligation, with all the kindred notions of the inherent authority of the Creator and the innate subordination of himself, the creature, of the aboriginal right of the Creator alone in all the creatures, and the utter absence of any right in himself to any other creature whatsoever. The command concerning this tree thus set his moral convictions a going, and awakened in him the new and pleasing consciousness that he was a moral being, and not a mere clod of the valley or brute of the field.

This is the first thing this tree did for man; and we shall find it would have done a still better thing for him if he had only made a proper use of it. Third. The absence of this tree would not at all have secured Adam from the possibility or the consequence of disobedience. Any grant to him whatsoever must have been made "with the reserve," implicit or explicit, of the rights of all others. "The thing reserved" must in equity have been made known to him. In the present course of things it must have come in his way, and his trial would have been inevitable, and therefore his fall possible. Now, the forbidden tree is merely the thing reserved. Besides, even if man had been introduced into a sphere of existence where no reserved tree or other thing could ever have come within the range of his observation, and so no outward act of disobedience could have been perpetrated, still, as a being of moral susceptibility, he must come to the acknowledgment, express or implied, of the rights of the heavenly crown, before a mutual good understanding could have been established between him and his Maker. Thus, we perceive that even in the impossible Utopia of metaphysical abstraction there is a virtual forbidden tree, which forms the test of a man's moral relation to his Creator. Now, if the reserve is necessary, and therefore the test of obedience inevitable, to a moral being, it only remains to inquire whether the test employed be suitable and seasonable.

Fourth. What is here made the matter of reserve, and so the test of obedience is so far from being trivial or out of place, as has been imagined, that it is the proper and the only object immediately available for these purposes. The immediate need of man is food. The kind of food primarily designed for him is the fruit of trees. Grain, the secondary kind of vegetable diet, is the product of the farm rather than of the garden, and therefore does not now come into use. As the law must be laid down before man proceeds to an act of appropriation, the matter of reserve and consequent test of obedience is the fruit of a tree. Only by this can man at present learn the lessons of morality. To devise any other means, not arising from the actual state of things in which man was placed, would have been arbitrary and unreasonable. The immediate sphere of obedience lies in the circumstances in which he actually stands. These afforded no occasion for any other command than what is given. Adam had no father, or mother, or neighbor, male or female, and therefore the second table of the law could not apply. But he had a relation to his Maker, and legislation on this could not be postponed. The command assumes the kindest, most intelligible, and convenient form for the infantile mind of primeval man.

Fifth. We are now prepared to understand why this tree is called the tree of the knowledge of good and evil. The prohibition of this tree brings man to the knowledge of good and evil. The products of creative power were all very good Gen 1:31. Even this tree itself is good, and productive of unspeakable good in the first instance to man. The discernment of merit comes up in his mind by this tree. Obedience to the command of God not to partake of this tree is a moral good. Disobedience to God by partaking of it is a moral evil. When we have formed an idea of a quality, we have at the same time an idea of its contrary. By the command concerning this tree man became possessed of the conceptions of good and evil, and so, theoretically, acquainted with their nature. This was that first lesson in morals of which we have spoken. It is quite evident that this knowledge could not be any physical effect of the tree, seeing its fruit was forbidden. It is obvious also that evil is as yet known in this fair world only as the negative of good. Hence, the tree is the tree of the knowledge of good and evil, because by the command concerning it man comes to this knowledge.

24. Webster's 1828 Dictionary
    Humanity
    HUMAN'ITY, n. [L. humanitas.]

    • The peculiar nature of man, by which he is distinguished from other beings. Thus Christ, by his incarnation, was invested with humanity.

    • Mankind collectively; the human race.

    • The kind feelings, dispositions and sympathies of man, by which he is distinguished from the lower orders of animals; kindness; benevolence; especially, a disposition to relieve persons in distress, and to treat with tenderness those who are helpless and defenseless; opposed to cruelty.

    • A disposition to treat the lower orders of animals with tenderness, or at least to give them no unnecessary pain.

    • The exercise of kindness; acts of tenderness.

    • Philology; grammatical studies.

    • Humanities, in the plural, signifies grammar, rhetoric and poetry; for teaching which there are professors in the universities of Scotland.

    Random House Dictionary

    Humanity:

    All human beings collectively; the human race, mankind. The quality or condition of being human.

Chapter 5 Consequences and Compassion

25. Gen 3:7
    Then the eyes of both of them were opened, and they knew that they were naked; and they sewed fig leaves together and made themselves loin coverings.

26. Strong's Hebrew and Greek Dictionaries
    Compassion

H7356
רחם
racham
rakh'-am

From H7355; compassion (in the plural); by extension the womb (as cherishing the foetus); by implication a maiden: - bowels, compassion, damsel, tender love, (great, tender) mercy, pity, womb.
G4697
σπλαγχνίζομαι
splagchnizomai
splangkh-nid'-zom-ahee

Middle voice from G4698; to have the bowels yearn, that is, (figuratively) feel sympathy, to pity: - have (be moved with) compassion.

Chapter 6   Revenge or Justice

27. Strong's Hebrew & Greek Dictionary
Revenge
H5358
נקם

nâqam
naw-kam'

A primitive root; to grudge, that is, avenge or punish: - avenge (-r, self), punish, revenge
(self), X surely, take vengeance.

28. Strong's Hebrew & Greek Dictionary
Righteousness H4941
מ‧שׁ‧פ‧ט
mishpâṭ
mish-pawt'

From H8199; properly a verdict (favorable or unfavorable) pronounced judicially, especially a sentence or formal decree (human or (particularly) divine law, individual or collectively), including the act, the place, the suit, the crime, and the penalty; abstractly justice, including a particular right, or privilege (statutory or customary), or even a style: - + adversary, ceremony, charge, X crime, custom, desert, determination, discretion, disposing, due, fashion, form, to be judged, judgment, just (-ice, -ly), (manner of) law (-ful), manner, measure, (due) order, ordinance, right, sentence, usest, X worthy, + wrong.

Justice H6664
צדק
tsedeq
tseh'-dek

From H6663; the right (natural, moral or legal); also (abstractly) equity or (figuratively) prosperity: - X even, (X that which is altogether) just (-ice), ([un-]) right (-eous) (cause, -ly, -ness).

29. Websters 1828 Dictionary on Curse
CURSE, v.t. pret. and pp. cursed or curst.
1.   1. To utter a wish of evil against one; to imprecate evil upon; to call for mischief or injury to fall upon; to execrate.

30. Strong's Hebrew and Greek Dictionary
Cursed
H779
ארר
'ârar
aw-rar'

A primitive root; to execrate: - X bitterly curse.

31. Webster's Dictionary 1828
Execrate
EX'ECRATE, v.t. [L. execror, from ex and sacer, the primary sense of which is to separate. See Sacred.]

Literally, to curse; to denounce evil against, or to imprecate evil on; hence, to detest utterly; to abhor; to abominate.

Random House Dictionary: Execrate – To detest utterly, abhor, abominate

To curse, imprecate evil upon

32. Matt Henry's Commentary on Gen 3:1-5 Genesis 3:1-5

Satan assaulted our first parents, to draw them to sin, and the temptation proved fatal to them. The tempter was the devil, in the shape and likeness of a serpent. Satan's plan was to draw our first parents to sin, and so to separate between them and their God. Thus the devil was from the beginning a murderer, and the great mischief maker. The person tempted was the woman: it was Satan's policy to enter into talk with her when she was alone. There are many temptations to which being alone gives great advantage; but the communion of saints tends very much to their strength and safety. Satan took advantage by finding her near the forbidden tree. They that would not eat the forbidden fruit, must not come near the forbidden tree. Satan tempted Eve, that by her he might tempt Adam. It is his policy to send temptations by hands we do not suspect, and by those that have most influence upon us. Satan questioned whether it were a sin or not, to eat of this tree. He did not disclose his design at first, but he put a question which seemed innocent. Those who would be safe, need to be shy of talking with the tempter. He quoted the command wrong. He spoke in a taunting way. The devil, as he is a liar, so he is a scoffer from the beginning; and scoffers are his children. It is the craft of Satan to speak of the Divine law as uncertain or unreasonable, and so to draw people to sin; it is our wisdom to keep up a firm belief of God's command, and a high respect for it. Has God said, Ye shall not lie, nor take his name in vain, nor be drunk, etc.? Yes, I am sure he has, and it is well said; and by his grace I will abide by it. It was Eve's weakness to enter into this talk with the serpent: she might have perceived by his question, that he had no good design, and should therefore have started back. Satan teaches men first to doubt, and then to deny. He promises advantage from their eating this fruit. He aims to make them discontented with their present state, as if it were not so good as it might be, and should be. No condition will of itself bring content, unless the mind be brought to it. He tempts them to seek preferment, as if they were fit to be gods. Satan ruined himself by desiring to be like the Most High, therefore he sought to infect our first parents with the same desire, that he might ruin them too. And still the devil draws people into his interest, by suggesting to them hard thoughts of God, and false hopes of advantage by sin. Let us, therefore, always think well of God as the best good, and think ill of sin as the worst evil: thus let us resist the devil, and he will flee from us.

33.   Strong's Hebrew and Greek Dictionary
Worrisomeness
H6093
עצ·בון
itstsâbôn
its-tsaw-bone'

From H6087; worrisomeness, that is, labor or pain: - sorrow, toil.
H6087
עצב

âtsab
aw-tsab'

A primitive root; properly to carve, that is, fabricate or fashion; hence (in a bad sense) to worry, pain or anger: - displease, grieve, hurt, make, be sorry, vex, worship, wrest.

(This word is usually translated – grieved)

34. Strong's Hebrew and Greek Dictionary
   H6089
   עצב
   etseb
   eh'-tseb

   From H6087; an earthen vessel; usually (painful) toil; also a pang (whether of body or mind): - grievous, idol, labor, sorrow.

35. Strong's Hebrew and Greek Dictionary
   H4910
   מש ל
   mâshal
   maw-shal'

   A primitive root; to rule: - (have, make to have) dominion, governor, X indeed, reign, (bear, cause to, have) rule (-ing, -r), have power.

Chapter 7   Guilt: the breaker or builder of relationships

36. Gen 1:27 (NAS)
   God created man in His own image, in the image of God He created him; male and female He created them.

37. Genesis 1:26-31 (NAS)
   Then God said, "Let Us make man in Our image, according to Our likeness; and let them rule over the fish of the sea and over the birds of the sky and over the cattle and over all the earth, and over every creeping thing that creeps on the earth." God created man in His own image, in the image of God He created him; male and female He created them. God blessed them; and God said to them, "Be fruitful and multiply, and fill the earth, and subdue it; and rule over

the fish of the sea and over the birds of the sky and over every living thing that moves on the earth." Then God said, "Behold, I have given you every plant yielding seed that is on the surface of all the earth, and every tree which has fruit yielding seed; it shall be food for you; and to every beast of the earth and to every bird of the sky and to everything that moves on the earth which has life, I have given every green plant for food"; and it was so. God saw all that He had made, and behold, it was very good. And there was evening and there was morning, the sixth day.

38. Albert Barnes Notes on the Bible
     Gen 1:28
     The divine blessing is now pronounced upon man. It differs from that of the lower animals chiefly in the element of supremacy. Power is presumed to belong to man's nature, according to the counsel of the Maker's will [Gen 1:26]. But without a special permission he cannot exercise any lawful authority. For the other creatures are as independent of him as he is of them. As creatures he and they are on an equal footing, and have no natural fight either over the other. Hence, it is necessary that he should receive from high heaven a formal charter of right over the things that were made foran. He is therefore authorized, by the word of the Creator, to exercise his power in subduing the earth and ruling over the animal kingdom. This is the meet sequel of his being created in the image of God. Being formed for dominion, the earth and its various products and inhabitants are assigned to him for the display of his powers. The subduing and ruling refer not to the mere supply of his natural needs, for which provision is made in the following verse, but to the accomplishment of his various purposes of science and beneficence, whether towards the inferior animals or his own race. It is the part of intellectual and moral reason to employ power for the ends of general no less than personal good. The sway of man ought to be beneficent.

39. Mark 7:20-23
     And He was saying, "That which proceeds out of the man, that is what defiles the man. "For from within, out of the heart of men, proceed the evil thoughts, fornications, thefts, murders, adulteries, deeds of coveting and wickedness, as well as deceit, sensuality, envy, slander, pride and foolishness. "All these evil things proceed from within and defile the man."

40. Romans 3:23-24
     for all have sinned and fall short of the glory of God, being justified as a gift by His grace through the redemption, which is in Christ Jesus;

41. Webster's 1828 Dictionary
    Guilt
    GUILT, n. gilt.

    Criminality; that state of a moral agent, which results from his actual
    commission of a crime or offense, knowing it to be a crime, or violation of law.
    To constitute guilt there must be a moral agent enjoying freedom of will, and
    capable of distinguishing between right and wrong, and a willful or intentional
    violation of a known law, or rule of duty. The guilt of a person exists, as soon as
    the crime is committed; but to evince it to others, it must be proved by
    confession, or conviction in due course of law. Guilt renders a person a debtor
    to the law, as it binds him to pay a penalty in money or suffering. Guilt
    therefore implies both criminality and liableness to punishment. Guilt may
    proceed either from a positive act or breach of law, or from voluntary neglect
    of known duty.

    2. Criminality in a political or civil view; exposure to forfeiture or other penalty.
    A ship incurs guilt by the violation of a blockade.

    Crime; offense

42. Oxfords readings in Philosophical theology, Volume 1, pages 295-297

    The guilt is objective guilt if the agent has failed to fulfill a moral obligation (or
    done an act obligatory not to do) whether or not he realized that this was his
    moral obligation or that he was failing in respect of it. I am objectively guilty
    for failing to educate my children properly even if I believe that I have no duty
    to educate my children or if I believe that sending them to a certain school,
    which unknown to me is totally incompetent, is educating my children
    properly. The guilt is subjective if the agent has failed to fulfill what he believes
    to be his moral obligation (or done what he believed to be obligatory not to
    do), whether or not there was such an obligation so long as the agent was free
    to do or refrain from doing the action, in whatever sense of "free" makes him
    morally responsible for that action.

    But the assertion that someone is guilty is not just an assertion about the past;
    it makes two further claims about the present. The worst is that the guilty one
    owes something to the one whom he has wronged, his victim. If I fail in an
    obligation, I do not just do a wrong, I do a wrong to someone. If I promise you
    that I will give a lecture and then do not turn up, or if I kick you in a fit of anger,

I have done a wrong to you. By hurting you, I put myself in a moral situation somewhat like the legal situation of a debtor who has failed to repay money borrowed from a bank. But the kind of debt owed by failure to perform one's moral obligations is often no mere financial one. Insofar as the victim is a person, that person is known personally to the wrongdoer, the failure is a failure of personal trust, and above all if there is ill-will (deliberate malice or negligence) on the part of the wrong-doer, then there is a totally new kind of harm involved the harm done to personal relations by a wrong attitude by the wrongdoer. Yet there is still more to moral guilt than past failure and present debt. Through his past failure the guilty one has acquired a negative status, somewhat like being unclean, which needs to be removed. By making a promise a person puts himself under certain obligations, but his status is in no way bad or unclean in consequence. There is more in the present to being guilty than incurring new obligations.

There is something wrong with a person even if his guilt is purely objective. If I unintentionally break your best vase or light the fire with the manuscript of your book, I acquire the status of a wrongdoer even if my actions were done in total ignorance of their nature or consequence (and even if I had taken all reasonable precautions to ensure that they had no such nature or consequence). It is, I suggest, a virtually unanimous moral intuition that this is so, that in such circumstances I acquire a status which needs purging by reparation if possible, and certainly by apology. This is because in interacting with my fellows, I undertake responsibility for seeing that certain things are done and certain things are not done (e.g., in holding your vase, I take responsibility for its not getting broken); and bad luck (my actions having bad consequences, despite my taking reasonable precautions) no more removes the responsibility, than it excuses you from repaying a man a sum of money which you have borrowed from him, even if you have that same amount stolen.

But of course the guilt is of a different kind if I knowingly fail in my obligations toward you if my guilt is subjective as well as objective. Here again I suggest that a virtually unanimous moral intuition suggests that far more is wrong, and far more needs doing to put it right. If I deliberately break your best vase, it is no good my saying "I really am very sorry." I have got to make several speeches distancing myself from the act and I have got to make reparation very quickly. I have wronged you so much the worse that my guilt is of a qualitatively different kind. The Book of Numbers differentiated between "sins committed unknowingly" and "sins committed with a high hand" (i.e., knowingly), declaring various kinds of ritual reparation suitable for the former and some very serious punishment for the latter. The reason for the vast difference is that when I deliberately break your best vase, I have failed not merely in my outward obligations toward you, but also in that attitude of purpose toward you which I owe you, the attitude of seeking no harm for you.

What if there is no objective guilt, but I fail in what I believe to be my obligations toward you? I try to break your best vase, but by accident break my own instead. Have I wronged you? My argument suggests that the answer is yes; and we can see that the answer is correct from considering more serious cases.

I try to kill you but the shot misses. From the obvious need for reparation of rather more than a short apology, we can see that wrong has been done and guilt acquired. Both subjective and objective guilt are stains on a soul requiring expunging; but subjective guilt is embedded in the soul while objective guilt lies on the surface.

43. Pastor Bruce Goettshe, Union Church of LaHarpe, (used by permission)

44. Strong's Hebrew & Greek Dictionary
G3670
oμολογέω
homologeō
hom-ol-og-eh'-o

From a compound of the base of G3674 and G3056; to assent, that is, covenant, acknowledge: - con- (pro-) fess, confession is made, give thanks, promise.

Chapter 8   Where are you?

45. Strong's Hebrew and Greek Dictionaries
H5375
נשׂא נסה
nâsâ' nâsâh
naw-saw', naw-saw'

A primitive root; to lift, in a great variety of applications, literally and figuratively, absolutely and relatively: - accept, advance, arise, (able to, [armor], suffer to) bear (-er, up), bring (forth), burn, carry (away), cast, contain, desire, ease, exact, exalt (self), extol, fetch, forgive, furnish, further, give, go on, help, high, hold up, honorable (+ man), lade, lay, lift (self) up, lofty, marry, magnify, X needs, obtain, pardon, raise (up), receive, regard, respect, set (up), spare, stir up, + swear, take (away, up), X utterly, wear, yield.

Chapter 9   Where Am I

46. Piaget, 1954

47. Stephen Pattison, 2000
    There is, therefore, an important distinction to be made between acute, reactive shame that occurs in particular situations, and chronic shame or shame proneness as a personality or character trait. The former is painful but temporary and limited in its effects, which by no means are all negative. While the characteristics of the latter are similar to those of the former – family resemblance again – they are extended in time and influence. They can cast a permanent shadow over a person's life, character, and personality. P. 83

48. Strong's Hebrew and Greek Dictionaries
    Ashamed
    H954
    בּ·וֹ·שׁ
    bûsh
    boosh

    A primitive root; properly to pale, that is, by implication to be ashamed; also (by implication) to be disappointed, or delayed: - (be, make, bring to, cause, put to, with, a-) shame (-d), be (put to) confounded (-fusion), become dry, delay, be long.

49. Strong's Hebrew and Greek Dictionaries
    Man
    H120
    אדם
    'âdâm
    aw-dawm'

    From H119; ruddy, that is, a human being (an individual or the species, mankind, etc.): - X another, + hypocrite, + common sort, X low, man (mean, of low degree), person.

H119
אדם
'âdam
aw-dam'

To show blood (in the face), that is, flush or turn rosy: - be (dyed, made) red (ruddy).

50. Eph 3:20 (NAS)
Now to Him who is able to do far more abundantly beyond all that we ask or think, according to the power that works within us,

Chapter 10   The Gift of Kidneys

51. In His Image Pg 73-80
No cell lies more than a hair's breadth from a blood capillary, lest poisonous by-products pile up and cause the same ill-effects demonstrated in the tourniquet experiment. Through a basic chemical process of gas diffusion and transfer, individual red blood cells drifting along inside narrow capillaries simultaneously release their cargos of fresh oxygen and absorb waste products (carbon dioxide, urea, and uric acid, etc.) from these cells. The red cells then deliver the hazardous waste chemicals to organs that can dump them outside the body. p. 75

52.   Encyclopedia of Human Biology
The average body for a 70 kg adult is about 42 liters, 60% of the body weight...

53. Webster's 1828 Dictionary
Repentance
REPENT'ANCE, n.

1. Sorrow for anything done or said; the pain or grief which a person experiences in consequence of the injury or inconvenience produced by his own conduct.

2. In theology, the pain, regret or affliction which a person feels on account of his past conduct, because it exposes him to punishment. This sorrow proceeding merely from the fear of punishment is called legal repentance, as

being excited by the terrors of legal penalties, and it may exist without an amendment of life.

3. Real penitence; sorrow or deep contrition for sin, as an offense and dishonor to God, a violation of his holy law, and the basest ingratitude towards a Being of infinite benevolence. This is called evangelical repentance, and is accompanied and followed by amendment of life.

Repentance is a change of mind, or a conversion from sin to God.

Godly sorrow worketh repentance to salvation. [2 Cor 7. Mat 3]

Repentance is the relinquishment of any practice, from conviction that it has offended God.

Chapter 11   Sweet Smell of Repentance

54.   Parirenal Fat – Greys Anatomy

Pg 1114 Grays Anatomy

The perirenal fascia is a multilaminated fascial layer that surround the kidney, suprarenal glands, upper ureter and assoiciated fat, which all lie in the perirenal space.

55. Gen 2:18
Then the LORD God said, "It is not good for the man to be alone; I will make him a helper suitable for him."

56. Vygotsky
Quoted in Educational Psychology, by Anita Woolfolk.
Vygotsky believed that human activities take place in cultural settings and that they cannot be understood apart from these settings. One of his key ideas was that our specific mental structures and processes can be traced to our interactions with others. These social interactions are more than simple influences on cognitive development – they actually create our cognitive structures and thinking processes. P. 55

57. Routman
Curriculum and standards must first connect with the lives and spirits of our children if we're to have any lasting success. Unless we reach into our students' hearts, we have no entry into their minds. Through drill and memorization, we can get students to complete assignments and pass tests.

But there is a price to pay for such short-term accomplishment. We will never inspire our students to learn for their own sake and to love coming to school. Bonding with our students is the "human essential," the intimately personal connection that is the core of responsive, excellent teaching. p. 12

58. Oxforddictionaries.com - Life - noun (plural lives /līvz/)
The condition that distinguishes animals and plants from inorganic matter, including the capacity for growth, reproduction, functional activity, and continual change preceding death.

Websters 1828 Dictionary - Life - n. plu lives. [See Live.]
1. In a general sense, that state of animals and plants, or of an organized being, in which its natural functions and motions are performed, or in which its organs are capable of performing their functions. A tree is not destitute of life in winter, when the functions of its organs are suspended; nor man during a swoon or syncope; nor strictly birds, quadrupeds or serpents during their torpitude in winter. They are not strictly dead, till the functions of their organs are incapable of being renewed.
2. In animals, animation; vitality; and in man, that state of being in which the soul and body are united.

59. Strong's Hebrew and Greek Dictionary
Compassion –   G4697

σπλαγχνίζομαι

splagchnizomai

splangkh-nid'-zom-ahee

Middle voice from G4698; to have the bowels yearn, that is, (figuratively) feel sympathy, to pity: - have (be moved with) compassion.

Chapter 12 Freedom

60. Mat 23:35
so that upon you may fall the guilt of all the righteous blood shed on earth, from the blood of righteous Abel to the blood of Zechariah, the son of Berechiah, whom you murdered between the temple and the altar.
Heb 11:4 By faith Abel offered to God a better sacrifice than Cain, through which he obtained the testimony that he was righteous, God testifying about his gifts, and through faith, though he is dead, he still speaks.

61. Gen 2:24

    For this reason a man shall leave his father and his mother, and be joined to his wife; and they shall become one flesh.

Bibliography

Barnes, Albert. *Notes on the bible.* New York: Harper and Brothers Publishers. 1854

Brand, Paul, and Yancey, Philip. *In His Image.* Judith Markham Books, Zondervan Publishing House, Grand Rapids, Michigan. 1984

C. S. Lewis. (n.d.). BrainyQuote.com. Retrieved May 18, 2013, BrainyQuote.com: http://www.brainyquote.com/quotes/quotes/c/cslewis141015.html

Clarke, A. *The Holy Bible with a commentary and critical notes, vol. 1.* Abingdon-Cokesbury Press, New York. 1851.

Cummings, E. Mark; Ballard, Mary; El-Sheikh, Mona; Lake, Margaret. *Influence of conflict between adults on the emotions and aggression of young children.* Developmental Psychology, Vol. 21 (3), May 1985. pp 495-507

Encyclopedia of human biology, vol. 1. Renato Dulbecco, editor in-chief. Academic Press, Inc. 1991.

Encyclopedia of human biology, vol. 3. Renato Dulbecco, editor in-chief. Academic Press, Inc. 1991.

Graham, Hicks, Shimmin & Thompson. *Biology: God's Living Creation.* Beka Books Publication. Pensacola Christian College, Pensacola, Florida, 1986.

Gray's Anatomy, 39th edition. Susan Standring editor in-chief. Elsevier, Churchill, Livingston, 2005.

Henry, Matthew. *Commentary on the whole bible, vol. 1.* New Modern Edition. Hendrickson Publishers, Inc.

Keil & Delitzsch. *Biblical commentary on the Old Testament, Vol. 1.* William B. Eerdman's Publishing Company. Grand Rapids, Michigan. Reprinted, November, 1983.

Life. (2013). oxforddictionaries.com. Retrieved June 17, 2013 from oxforddictionaries.com.
http://oxforddictionaries.com/definition/english/life?q=life

Living. (2013). 1828mshaffer.com. Retreived June 17, 2013 from mshaffer.com
Web site. http://1828.mshaffer.com/d/search/word,living

Oxford English dictionary, 2nd edition. Prepared by J.A. Simpson and E.S.C. Weiner.
Clarendon Press, Oxford. 1998,

Oxford readings in philosophical theology, volume 1. Edited by Michael Rea.
Oxford University Press, 2009.

Pattison, Stephen. *Shame: theory, therapy, theology.* Cambridge University Press,
2000.

Piaget, J. (1954). *The construction of reality in the child* (M. Cook, Trans.) New
York, NY: Basic Books.

Piaget, J. (1964). Development and Learning. In R. Ripple &V. Rockcastle (Eds.),
Piaget rediscovered (pp. 7-20),. Ithaca, NY: Cornell University Press.

Piaget, J. (1985). *The equilibrium of cognitive structures: The central problem of
intellectual development* (T. Brown & K.L. Thampy, Trans.). Chicago, IL: University of
Chicago Press.

Random house unabridged dictionary, 2nd edition. Random House, New York. 1993.

Ratey, John. *Spark: The revolutionary new science of exercise and the brain.* Little,
Brown and Company, 2008.

Routman, Regie (2003). *Reading Essentials: the specifics you need to teach reading
well.* Heinemann, Portsmouth, NH.

Strong, James. *The new strong's complete dictionary of bible words.* Thomas
Nelson Publishers, 1996.

Vygotsky, L.S. (1978). *Mind in society: The development of higher mental process.*
Cambridge, MA: Harvard University Press.

Woolfolk, Anita. *Educational Psychology,* 12th edition. Pearson Education, Inc.
Boston, Massachusetts.

About The Authors

Dr. Jim and Malinda Uhlenkott have been married for 40 years. They have raised four children and have eight grandchildren (so far).

Dr. Jim Uhlenkott earned his Ph.D. in Educational Leadership from Gonzaga University, in Spokane, Washington. He has taught as a classroom teacher for the Mead School District outside Spokane, Washington, been a professor at Gonzaga University, Director of Undergraduate Education at Eastern Washington University, and is currently a Visiting Professor of Education at Whitworth University.

Malinda Uhlenkott earned her B.S. in Biology from Eastern Washington University, has worked at veterinarian clinics and currently owns and maintains several rental homes.

Jim and Malinda have spent their entire adult lives working with and teaching children and young adults. They directed two summer camps, one for diabetic children, and worked as directors for the Master's Commission Discipleship Program for Young Adults, both in the United States and in Bratislava, Slovakia.

Made in the USA
Charleston, SC
23 June 2014